more than than soil more than sky

QUERCUS
Review
P R E S S

more than soil more than sky

EDITED BY
SAM PIERSTORFF
GILLIAN WEGENER
STELLA BERATLIS
ED BEARDEN

PHOTOGRAPHS BY
DOUG HOLCOMB

THE MODESTO POETS

Quercus Review Press, one of the only community college presses in the United States, is committed to inspiring and enriching lives within its community and around the world through its poetry publications. Its activities are supported by the Modesto Junior College Foundation, the Department of English at Modesto Junior College, and by philanthropic contributions from individuals. For more information, visit www.quercusreview.com.

QUERCUS REVIEW PRESS
MODESTO, CA

More Than Soil, More Than Sky: The Modesto Poets
Copyright © 2011, Quercus Review Press
All rights revert to individual authors upon publication.

Published by Quercus Review Press, Department or English, Modesto Junior College, 435 College Ave. Modesto, CA 95350

Edited by Sam Pierstorff, Gillian Wegener, Stella Beratlis, Ed Bearden
Photographs by Doug Holcomb
Cover Design by Claire Zoghb
Interior Design by Quercus Review Press

Library of Congress Control Number: 2011935952
ISBN-13: 978-1466200678
ISBN-10: 1466200677

First Printing

Printed in the United States of America

10 9 8 7 6 5 4 3 2 1

—This book is dedicated to the memory of Lee Nicholson,
teacher, poet, friend.

contents | more than soil, more than sky

THE MODESTO POETS

FOREWORD_____

The geographer William Preston has said that if the Great Central Valley of California were anywhere else in the world, it would be considered one of the cradles of civilization. I have always liked this perception, not just because I believe him, but because I know a levy road at the San Luis National Wildlife Refuge from which I can see the curving rampart of the Diablo Range to the west and the snow-dusted rim of the Sierra Nevada to the east, and feel the physical, enclosing comfort of a cradle, of a protected, fecund valley. The image also appeals to me because a cradle usually holds something alive and stirring, some bawling newness clamoring for attention. Modesto finds itself almost in the middle of this cradle and this anthology of poetry, *More Than Soil, More Than Sky,* is the latest communal baby.

Modesto, relatively recent and modest spawn of the railroad, is located between two tributaries (the Tuolumne and Stanislaus) of the once mighty, and now reviving, San Joaquin River, flowing south to north into the Delta, where the stream's many channels and sloughs meet those of its sister river, the Sacramento. It is important to keep in mind Modesto's location, not just because grizzlies on the banks of the Tuolumne once outnumbered poets (and poets constantly need to be reminded of their position in the food chain), but because the fertility of a landscape created by rivers, spilling rainfall and snowmelt, created a place of astounding floral and faunal diversity: riparian gallery forests and freshwater marshes, oak woodlands and broad savannas. The productivity of the landscape, the richness of what John Muir called "bee pastures" (Valley grasslands), gave rise to one of the densest native populations north of the Valley of Mexico. The first peoples of this area, the Miwok and Northern Valley Yokuts, were shaped by a landscape of breathtaking lyrical power and drama, and their reverence for the life-giving earth and sky moved them to compose stories, songs and dances, and to elaborate rites of thanksgiving and propitiation, long before the poetry of this place was expressed in Spanish or English. It is good to remember that the first cruising in Modesto was done not in low riders but in tule balsas.

There's a lot of poetry where the wild things are and many of the poems in *More Than Soil, More Than Sky* testify to the enduring telluric powers of our region. The persistence of a deep emotional bond to place, an attitude of reverence and affection, is a constant, as is the region's cultural diversity (or what poet Angela Salinas describes as "this crazy mix of languages, peoples, ideas"). Many of the poets in this anthology are from elsewhere, but the *numina*, or local spirits, find them when they pay heed, and speak through them of displacement, sorrow, beauty, magic. Modesto is, for better or worse, a city of the rural California heartland. Much of the natural diversity of its environs has been replaced by agricultural diversity and urbanization, often fueled by the labor of various immigrant groups, but what remains and what is being restored remains quickening. This land and its denizens feed us, literally and imaginatively, and the poets here write about vernal pools and canneries, yellow-billed magpies and farm wives, wild oats and donut shops. Here you can still be surprised by a spadefoot toad hatch, bugling and jousting elk, families of sandhill cranes. And, if you're lucky, a coyote may stop, sit down and listen to your complaints about the world.

If the Tuolumne reminds us of our debt to mountain snowpacks, the Stanislaus, named after the Yokuts Indian leader and rebel, Estanislao, reminds us that our county (only one of three named after a California Indian leader) has also been a place of rebellion, historical turmoil and violence. Valley Indians were regarded as troublemakers because they fought for survival against cultural systems bent on destroying them. The statue of Estanislao in front of the County Courthouse at 11th and I streets in Modesto raises his hand as if he would like to stop the traffic, history, us. He creates a bridge between deep historical time and the problems and tensions of the current day. Some of the best poems in the anthology address the problems we often do not want to see: the demoralizing experience of extended unemployment ("A Year Out of Work"), the cost of war ("A Soldier's Thoughts: Before Breakfast," "Fallujah Station"), prostitution on Ninth Street ("I Didn't Know They Sold That at the Farmers' Market"), human weeds ("Green Thumb"), the devaluing of people we depend on and exploit but "do not love back" ("California Love Song").

If poetry is the most vital counter-force to *Homo economicus* and poets the "unacknowledged legislators of the world," then *More Than Soil, More Than Sky* is testimony that Modesto is in the process of replacing street drugs with a powerful mental drug, with "that great accelerator of the mind" and liberator: the autonomous, unfettered word. It is impossible to exaggerate the role of Modesto teachers and Modesto Junior College in creating this cultural climate. At least two dozen poets in this volume are or have been teachers (Bearden, Beratlis, Crawford, Hamilton, Hansen, Haskett, Herrick, Johnson, Kantro, Keriotis, Myers, Neumann, Nicholson, Pierstorff, Preston, Robert, Rogers, Salerno, Salinas, Scheller, Thomas, Vallee, Wegener, Wright). Student diversity at community colleges makes for a more reciprocal relationship between teachers and students. As Bryce Thornburg writes, he was "directionless but surrounded by intelligent and supportive people." Teachers provide direction and tools for advocacy, students—inspiration. The teachers are there to encourage but also, in Ted

Orland's words, "to administer an occasional kick in the butt to flawless but stagnant work." No ivory tower here. In the community college classroom are eerily silent returning soldiers, the suddenly unemployed or estranged, people with learning disabilities, immigrants hungry for language, gang members just out of prison trying to steer their lives to a different course. They teach us back. They teach us patience and compassion. As Kay Ryan, national poet laureate and champion of community colleges has stated, "poetry makes great claims on the mind" and when teachers fuse their art with an art that fosters exhilaration and liberation, poetry arises in surprising places.

Modesto has been assembling the poetic materials of its identity for a long time. The City of Modesto sponsors annual poetry events, supports poets laureate, and has had cultural commissioners active on editorial boards of The Poets of the San Joaquin and Chaparral Poets. Poetry editor Tina Driskill has devoted a page to local poetry in each issue of *Stanislaus Connections*. Former Modesto poet laureate and teacher Sam Pierstorff has galvanized the young people of the region to attend his classes, Slam on Rye monthly poetry slams, and the annual ILL List slam in DROVES. Award-wining poet and teacher Gillian Wegener brings diverse, and sometimes, mildly antagonistic poetry cliques together at the Barkin' Dog every second Tuesday of the month and has succeeded in making them listen to one another and to poets from other parts of California. For three years photographers Dave Schroeder and Diane Moody created collaborative "collisions" between poets and photographers. Current poet laureate Ed Bearden has teamed up with microbiologist Richard Anderson to record interviews and readings by local poets to broadcast on local television and the worldwide web. And of course, this anthology is posthumously dedicated to Lee Nicholson—poet, teacher and listener without equal—whose admonition to "enter" poetry, that feral garden, and to "ease," leaving behind the mall and wanton destruction of people and places, speaks to us more forcefully than ever before.

This is a vibrant, cross-pollinating community in which older, sober poets become a lot wilder and younger ones a little more judicious. It is a community that emphasizes cultural participation over consumption and strives to speak for "those who are often silent." The new baby in this cradle is just beginning to wail and clamor and yes, sometimes, stink. But how we raise this infant will tell us who we are. Will poetry in Modesto make the city and the world a better place? Will it create a society capable of being moved by beauty and injustice? Will it make us more generous and inclusive? The answer, dear reader, is in your hands.

—Lillian Vallee

Thinking of Lee

In 1999, I gave my first poetry reading along with Gary Thomas at the much-missed Bookstore in McHenry Village. I knew most of the people there, but I did not know the smiling man in the wheelchair. Poetry readings are usually quiet affairs, but while I read, this man clapped his hands and hummed and exclaimed happily. His joy in the event was complete and intense, and I now know that it was his love of poetry, his love of image and rhythm, and his love of community that made him so joyful. He was truly and completely in love with language, and whether that language was a poem or the text on a box of Cheerios (I have evidence of this), Lee Nicholson was head over heels for language and always, always willing to share that love with others.

Lee was so generous to the poets in our area and beyond, listening, critiquing, encouraging, offering his own work to read, and rejoicing in the responses of others. Whether his role was that of a teacher at Turlock High School in the late 50s and early 60s or as a long-time teacher at MJC, Lee was a cheerleader for poets and poetry and for other writing he loved. His style wasn't everyone's cup of tea, but there was no denying that this man was passionate about his subject matter, and in talking with colleagues and former students and fellow poets and Lee's family, there is no denying that the impact he has had is broad and long-lasting.

For me, that impact is multi-faceted. Lee's encouragement made me more confident in my own work. He made me try harder to give useful feedback to others' work. And he made it very clear, through both the great joy he took in the world around him and in the humor lurking in so many of his poems, that poetry does not always need to be Serious Business, that it can be wondrous, that it can be funny, that anything that delights—an envelope with 39 one-cent bird stamps on it sent by a fellow poet, a crocheted tea cup found in a consignment store—can instigate a poem worthy of attention and revision and often of an elaborate presentation.

Lee was the embodiment of creativity in our area. Not only did he write, but he illustrated many of his works with his own collages and paintings and beautiful calligraphy. Lee believed that the whole package, the poem and the paper the poem was printed on and the way that poem was presented to the world, counted as a work of art, and he made it so. During his last hospital stay this early spring, Lee's sisters agreed that Lee would not want to live in the world if he could not create, and I could only nod in agreement. Creativity was Lee's sustenance, and it is lucky for those of us he has left behind that we have so much of his work to read and to admire and to be inspired by and, especially, to remember him by.

It is with that in mind that we dedicate this book to Lee Nicholson, teacher, poet and friend. We are pleased to be able to do this for him, to acknowledge his place in the lives of the writers in our community. Lee's physical presence is gone, but his place in our community, in the writing lives of the poets and in the teaching lives of those who carry on sharing their love and enthusiasm for poetry with new generations, will remain.

—Gillian Wegener

LEE NICHOLSON

Lee Nicholson is a native of the Great Central Valley. Born in Hanford in 1936, he spent his early years there, moving to Arkansas when he was a boy. He attended Little Rock Junior College, graduating with an AA degree in 1955; Millsaps College in Jackson, Mississippi, graduating with his BA in 1957; and the University of Mississippi, graduating with an MA in 1959. He later returned to California, where he earned a teaching credential in 1960 and went on to teach English at Turlock High School.

"In 1964, Lee became an instructor at Modesto Junior College, where he remained for the next 32 years as a beloved and inspirational teacher of the literary arts, especially poetry, as well as the history of antiques. Lee brought his love for literature and language back again and again to his students in Modesto, influencing generations of poets and writers with his passionate teaching and generous spirit. He also shared that generous spirit with the students of Yellville-Summit High School, his mother's alma mater, where he established the Retha Alice Medley Nicholson Prize in 2001 to recognize excellence in writing. Known for both his poetry and his calligraphy, Lee authored two books, *Common Ground* in 2000 and *Speakeasy* in 2005. Lee dealt with many health issues in the last years of his life, but continued to write poetry and take joy in the world around him. He passed away in March of 2011."

WATER, WEALTH…

High over city traffic with such grace
Curves a metal arch which supports a sign.
Its message hanging there in open space
Reads WATER, WEALTH, CONTENTMENT, HEALTH—a fine
      Combination of abstraction and price.
      They all depend in this hot, arid land
      On one element—Water—the blue bride
      Of Sky. For each daily wedding this band
Of iron surrounds with ceremony all
Those other essences—earth, sunlight, air.
A witness to all this cosmic dance and brawl
It stands. All lovers, fighters too, should stare.
      Look up. See through. Like some great Buddha's ring
      An arch can show a space or everything.

TWO DAYS TUMBLED IN WATER

1. At Venice

Ocean whitecaps turn back
and drain, gasping,
toward land.

From St. Mark's Square
pigeons whirl away
and away.

For just this moment
boys have put down
their toy violins.

Now Venice—
because she must—
it is her velvet habit—
floods.

The flow makes us all one—
silk and self—
shiver and burn.

2. Yosemite

And now at hand
on this nearby river—
the Upper Merced—
a downward light
slants, then blinds.
in summer, the skin
of water is warmer
than mine.

For a large minute

the steam and I—
confused—
changed hearts.

YOUR TEETH FLASH

The way to enter this poem is to
Turn your back on all taxes, houses, burn
All plastic, drop your dollars, throw each shoe,
Walk without a map, laugh, refuse to learn,
        Find a green grove with a central clearing,
        Stand naked until the sun sets your hair
        Afire, settle on one haunch and, hearing
        A bird totally free, sing to it, bare
Your heart, leave nothing out, murmur, cry.
Now you are the poem itself, the same,
And I love you. Your teeth flash. You can't die.
My poem, I love you, your doubtful fame.
        Now just once look back at me before you
        Go—lover, smoke and mirror, actor, cue.

WHEN BETH FELL IN LOVE WITH A RETIRED GENTLEMAN

Our retirement center rep is still finishing business
so she makes sounds like a good pal.
She points out nine rules of the place:
        Thou shalt not steal away.
        Do not feed the animals.
        Though shalt not have any images of graves.
        Luncheon is served at 11:28, dinner at 4:39.
        Thou shalt not stab residents in our elevator.
        Thou shalt not bear false peanuts.
        Do not covet thy neighbor's elephant.
        Thou shalt not own shovels.
        Rose-colored glasses must be worn at all times.
She points out how our pink glasses
change brown halls into a sunset design.
Our skin tones seem healthy.
All around are hundreds of plastic plants
dangling in Babylonian plenty,
our hanging gardens,
although only one of us
will ever use hanging plants
so gravely,
so plumb,
so vertical,
so literal.

Words gush from her whitely, soothing, like shaving cream.
She explains that a retirement center,
Once an elephant zoo,
For investors with vision,
Can become like this place of love.
Down from the halls we move, whiffs of dung
Rising from the thresholds. Ominous.
Smells you can see.
There she is, earth's biggest beast,

Elephant filling up space, air.
Elephant has been around a long time.
The sales rep warns that Elephant is never to be named
out loud—Death—as the word here is an obscenity,
unspeakable. Call her Beth.
So Elephant becomes my Beth.
Her breath, though a poison,
is soft, as real as her daily
pampering.

Beth whimpers.
She likes me.
She has been lonely.
The sales rep sees it is time to leave.
She pronounces,
"Little children, love one another,"
We give one another the eye,
human, elephant.
The beast already is eager with love.

SEVEN SIGNS I LOVE, I TRUST

Solitary whistling,

A face stilled after speech,

The flowing outward the flower,
snakelike and smooth from its mother soil,

The etiquette of spaces on trees
observed between birds,

Confessions of the body, unplanned,
emotional,

The gospel of the moon,

Uncertain ecstasies of time—

These spread rose-like.

"IN 'N' OUT" WITH METHUSELAH

St. Peter was in a cross mood.
He kept checking his Rolex and tapping his golden
     clipboard,
Useful tools here on the Outside, must like handguns
     or violins below.

When Methuselah finally showed up at the Pearly Gate,
Peter (called here "The Rock,"
Someone who could wrestle muscle against muscle
With the best) glared at this old man
And asked "What took you so long?"
Peter was not smiling.
Past the sapphire fence,
A purple like a sunset in Vegas,
Methuselah could see some of the great rides of
     Plausible Paradise.
Spirits waited in long lines.
He waved at Adam, who ignored him.
(Adam was still flirting with Eve,
Her face newly wet with sweet cider.)

"What took you so long?" the Rock asked again.
"I wanted to beat the record, sir," Methuselah admitted.
Peter (the Rock) was scribbling on his glittering board
"VANITY," one more grave infraction.

"This one does not learn. Bring back the parole board.
Oh, and bring some snowballs, 969 of them."
A plump secretary angel, kind of a blond helicopter,
Flew around in spirals.
Rock scratched again:
"HARD TIME." This was serious.

ONE-EARED AND FAMOUS

Let mere Theo see small and simple.

For Vincent any moon can lurch or dance.
No Cyclops he,
Van Gogh surveys in broader waverings
like a man drunk and staggering
between two tellings of truth,
stars spilling nightward,
yellow crossing darkest blue.

Beauty requires two silver selves,
Romulus and Remus from birth
clutching knives and aiming
for a brother's famous heart.

more
than
soil more
than
sky
THE
MODESTO
POETS

ANN W. BAILEY

Ann W. Bailey is a local writer and teacher who is pleased to applaud the persistent swell of creative commitment in this community and to participate whenever she can. She has contributed to regional periodicals and a variety of collaborations including: *Collision III: The Impact of Poetry and Photography, Asilomar 2011: Valley Sierra Arts Project,* Stockton's *In the Moment: A Music, Dance and Spoken Word* event, and dance and poetry collaborations with Stockton choreographer Lisa Rie at the SF Legion of Honor Dancing Poetry Festival. She writes with the Licensed Fools, a local writing group.

"I love the rural edges of this area, especially during golden hour or the blue-lit, early hours before dawn. It drives me to paint portraits and write landscapes."

STOCKTON REDS

My father would peel them, Stockton Reds,
and eat them like apples, leaning
against Joe Brandenburg's truck
Come blue dark, my mother
would stand on the shoulder of the levee, barefoot
except for Zori's, skirt snapping
and gaze out over acres of onions—
rippling tides of lacy white blooms
Winters later, missing them both
I plant Stockton Reds purposefully, pushing
my thumb into dark soil—
patting them snug into bed
There's no delta breeze in suburbia
but green shoots spindle up nonetheless,
Come summer, I eat them straight from the garden,
sweet and robust, peeling back parchment
shaking loose dirt from the roots;
Second crop seeds into moon stalks—
papery crowns with pips—
I gaze out my window at the white blooms
small ocean, landlocked in memory,
barefoot at the sink.

KAREN BAKER

Karen Baker writes with several writing groups in the Modesto area. She has been published in several journals and anthologies including *In the Grove*, *Rattlesnake Review*, *A Book of Common Fools*, and *Song of the San Joaquin*. She is a former editor of *hardpan, a journal of poetry*. Her chapbook, *Vocal Exercises in Stone,* was published by Rattlesnake Press in 2005. She was born in New York City and grew up in Rockford, Illinois.

"Italian cypress are amusing when the wind comes up. There is a procession of them, bobbing their pointed heads like priests reciting litanies near my home. They are immigrants like the ever present live oak, the eucalyptus, the re-channeled water, the dust bowl survivors, and many like me who thought they were passing through for a short visit, and landed here for most of a lifetime. As with any landscape, the valley and the city of Modesto changes with the perception of the viewer. I like to write sitting near the river or, most often, at my computer next to my back door, looking out on crepe myrtle and magnolia. Sometimes my writing landscape is a group of passionate poets sharing tea or valley wine and, always, words.

THE FORSAKEN CHINESE MERCHANT'S WIFE

Mud and moths define your garden
You enter like a distracted ghost
wandering as moss hangs from magnolia,
grazing your face in its tattered musings

His name passed through you only once this morning,
as dry wooden wind chimes clacked, as doves mourned
Your mind held court with wishes that were more like
        battle strategies;
escape plans, preparations of poisons

But these imaginings did not have to do with him anymore
They were gestures, habits of a certain desolation
Longing was yours, and ritual,
stiff reverence towards a predictable day

You are wife to a specter now,
submitting to this stark architecture of time
as you did to him once, inside a pale pink spring

PEARLED SOUL

Layered, opaque,
Brine born.
Mother, open your
Oyster mouth.

> Jet stream consciousness,
> Exhausting.
> Imitation clouds
> Zipper my sky.

Fuel gauge:
Quarter tank

In diligence we fall upon ourselves.
In grace we catch our footing.
I am blind to that old irritation.
I sit eating almonds, eye shaped.

> Biggest influence this week:
> Cornel West
> In discussions of Dostoyevsky,
> Carrying Ruskin to desert islands.

Fuel gauge:
Nearly full

The laboratory bends
Glass into ideas,
Recognizes the most useful truth,
Seizes it, white coated.

> Fuel gauge:
> Useless at light speed.

SEAN BARNETT

Sean Barnett's most recent poems have appeared in *Snail Mail Review, BlackCatPoems.com,* and the *MJC Celebration of the Humanities* anthology, 2010 and 2011.

"After graduating from Escalon High School in 2002, I enlisted in the US Army as an Infantryman. I was deployed under Operation Iraqi Freedom and Operation Enduring Freedom in both Iraq and Afghanistan. Once I completed my commitment with the military, I returned home to Modesto and started attending Modesto Junior College (MJC). My inspiration to write first took off while I was deployed to Iraq in 2003. My writing did not take on any real structure until I began working my way through the English classes at MJC. I occasionally attend the *Slam on Rye* poetry slams and I never miss the annual *Ill List* poetry slam invitational, which I was honored to judge last year. I frequently go to the Barkin' Dog Grill readings and I have read during its open mic a handful of times."

A SOLDIER'S THOUGHTS: BEFORE BREAKFAST

You weren't the first,
God knows you weren't the last

Of all the others,
Your mark stays with me

It was the shot,
I never should've taken

And every morning since,
It's your eyes I see

The death of you,
Has become the life of me

BORN INTO IT

I was born the year grandpa died,
Like my father, they gave me his name.

When dad died, they put a flag over him.
Dressed in blue, six giants, with stone faces,
Came and carried him away.

When Sergeant Martinez died, we put a flag over him.
Dressed in blue, I couldn't keep a stone face.
I bet I looked like a giant,
to his little boy.

Ed Bearden

Ed Bearden was editor of *The Sentinel*, the then Stanislaus State literary magazine in 1956-66. He has served as the state president of the California Federation of Chaparral Poets, received the 2007 Literary Arts Award presented by the Stanislaus Arts Council, and two Pushcart Prize nominations. He is the fifth Poet Laureate for the city of Modesto.

"I was born in Ceres in 1940 and grew up on a peach ranch. I spent three years in the Army, most of that time at the United States Military Academy at West Point, New York, as a medic. I received a graduate degree in social work in 1970 and taught sociology for two years. I am a licensed Marriage Family and Child Counselor and Real Estate Broker. My wife and I own our own real estate company, Choice Investments Realty. I retired after 24 years with Stanislaus County, most of that time as a child welfare supervisor. In 1983 I was elected to the Empire School Board and served 24 years. With the exception of my work in child welfare, each of these landscapes and experiences has found its way into my poetry. This is especially true of the orchards, rivers, canals, canneries and railroads. The odors are especially sharp: water as it sinks into dry ground, the husks of walnuts, the mud at Modesto Reservoir, gunpowder from a Thanksgiving pheasant hunting trip and the feel of peach-fuzz, hot and sticky and itchy-itchy-itchy."

FLIGHT ZONE VIETNAM

It is the air you remember.
The air you test with your finger
and your breath.
You need to know
its speed and direction.
You need to know the contents
of the air, that strange smell
you must identify, for the air
is all that you have as you fly.
It is your home away from home,
your home away from everything.

You never taste the air
without tasting her thighs.
Her flesh against the stubble
of your beard—a tough stubble.
She never complained.
It was all you had, all she had.
You took it, grabbed it
and every time you fly she
is there—her skin on the stubble
of your face. Its aroma fills
your nostrils. Whatever you
find in the air that does not
have her smell does not belong
is not safe, not what you fight
for, not what you fly for
as you fly through air thick

with fear, thick with separation
and the green bile of combat.

Then, in the heat of it, when
no action is safe and all are suspect
someone brings the dead

or news of the dead
and there is only death.

The taste of her nipples
disappears in the taste of vomit
that fills your mouth
and smothers her thigh
against the stubble of your cheek
hides behind the slick sheen
of sweat around your mouth
as you lick fear from your lips
like milk from her breasts
in this moment when nothing
is understood.

THE SONG OF THE MEADOWLARK

Spring can always be found in the
song of the meadowlark. First,
there is a clear high single note.
Then, even to one with an untrained
ear, the notes seem to blend as they
descend the scale. The meadowlark
sings a regional song with slight
but significant differences. But the
cry of the killdeer is the same
everywhere and when threatened
killdeer feign injury, become impaired,
crippled birds, dragging a broken wing
in the dirt; dragging and crying. It's
a throaty cry. A gurgle of vulnerability
that leads skunks or opossums away
from a nest hidden in short grasses.

Built on the ground, the nest is exposed,
its only protection pretense
                —a mother's masquerade.
Mothers everywhere watch the killdeer
and marvel. At night when they are
sleeping, it is not the song of the meadowlark
that comforts them in their sleep, but the nest
of the killdeer, where they send the hearts
            of their children.

THE PSYCHOTHERAPIST

There was always a box of Kleenex
on the table   beside the chair
in the room where we talked.
It was   as if   he knew
that sometime during our fifty-minute hour
I would notice them
discover they were there
hesitate before taking one.
Then... a long second to look at it
examine it
—as if it were a leaf and I a child again.

SILENCE

Listen.
Then listen closely.
You may
hear a car passing
or a passerby
say to a companion,
"What a fine day."
The rumble
of a truck may
sound like thunder.
Now find a nature spot,
where birds mutter
—then fly. When
the sky empties
you hear nothing.
Nothing always
makes you think
of something.

RELATIONSHIPS

Even when the
words are civil
and polite
things
may not
seem right.

Distance can be felt,
hangs not like
a bridge suspended
by ropes but
like the ropes
themselves.

It is as if the knots
that held them
have slipped
and all that once
seemed solid
is left dangling.

ROBERTA BEARDEN

Roberta Bearden is President of the Poets of the San Joaquin. She is a past state treasurer for the California Federation of Chaparral Poets, Inc. Roberta is on the editorial board of the *Song of the San Joaquin*. She has been published in the *Modesto Poets Corner, Song of the San Joaquin, Quercus Review,* and has won poetry contests statewide.

"I moved to Modesto when I was 9 years old, grew up swimming in dirt canals and dragging Tenth and Eleventh streets as a teenager. I learned to drive on a narrow country lane called Lincoln Avenue in East Modesto, bordered by peach orchards. Today, Lincoln is a four lane road, bordered by houses. It was not this early Modesto that influenced my writing, but the Modesto of my adulthood, sprawling, houses replacing orchards, streets paving over the best farmland in the world. It was the loss of this beautiful valley that made me sad, made me long for the simple life of childhood. I wrote my first poem when I was 36 but didn't really start writing poetry regularly until my late forties. Today I write poetry about events that happen both in Modesto and in the world. Events like Hurricane Katrina, and the friends I have made through Memorial Hospital's cancer services and the losses that come with age. Writing helps me work through these events that bring both pain and happiness. Writing reminds me how lucky I am to live in Modesto."

FOG

Fog shrouds the sleeping street.
Trees, bare of summer sunscreen,
struggle to pierce the silent blanket.

It creeps to the front door.
Traverses an open window,
slithers across the hushed terrace
—a lightly stepping stalker.

A THOUSAND MILES AWAY

I never met her, never held her hand.
I only talked to her once on the phone.

She had a low and melodious voice
and a quick wit. Her mind—caught in
a body where arms and legs no longer
functioned—was obviously sharp.

We talked a long time on the phone
until the winds of the hurricane silenced
the connection and the waters crept
silently through her doors and windows.

Stella Beratlis_____

Stella Beratlis lives in Modesto and teaches English at Modesto Junior College. Her poems have appeared in *Quercus Review, Song of the San Joaquin, hardpan, Penumbra,* and *The Place That Inhabits Us: Poems of the San Francisco Bay Watershed*, among others.

"When my family moved from Pleasanton to Modesto, I was surprised to find a place that was populated by cowboy boot-clad people, endless orchards, and irrigation canals. Here, the fog was so thick on some mornings that I was unsure if I were walking to school or disappearing, step by nervous step, into a misty cloud-world. Naturally, like many other kids who attended Beyer High, I couldn't wait to leave the area when I graduated in 1982—in search of culture, beauty, and residents with liberal attitudes. In my twenties, I lived in the Bay Area, New Orleans, Boston, and elsewhere, but little did I know that somehow the straight lines of the planted rows had become imprinted in my imagination and that I might feel genuinely glad to return from wherever else I'd been. In living and writing in Modesto for

the past 15 years, I've learned to pay attention to the lovely as well as the unlovely places that exist here. Sometimes it's hard to do when many Modesto landscapes seem more desolate or post-industrial than natural. But when I drive north on McHenry, the almond orchards, with their San Joaquin snow in early spring, remind me of where to look and how to see."

ORANGE GROVE RV PARK

The monarchs are migrating this spring
Larry has washed them off the windshield several times
at rest stops between Modesto and Bakersfield
and now he carefully scrapes the brazen expanse
again—the third time—at this RV park,
where the shtick is all-you-can-pick
oranges. The smell overwhelms as we pull in—
the narcotic scent of citrus honey only adults seem able
to detect. My mother inhales and moans, rapturous,
as my daughter shrieks, *I can't smell it I can't smell it,*
her dismay squeezing the air out of my chest like
a very tight hug. Some time later, with Larry still ministering
to the glass, we collect citrus blooms, follow a lizard
along a stack of railroad ties, and analyze how we might play
on an oversized concrete pipe randomly placed in sand.
The heat and exhaustion scour me clean. Above,
a helicopter buzzes in ever-widening circles in
weak yellow skies, a manhunt in neighboring groves.
The windshield is now filmed with new dust.
I sit on a picnic table, its flakes of blue paint
catching the weft of my pants, while the generations
who sandwich my life skip and slide, *korai*
in the sun-baked gravel, maidens in the trailer park.

CROP ROWS IN AUTUMN

This is how faces fall apart:
our eyes fixed to a point

somewhere on the flat horizon.
We walk in furrows of rich soil

for years, for a lifetime—
then start following the furrows

up to the clouds. This is how lives
fall open: a man loves and hopes

while his wife shrinks
one acre per year. How love

weaves out: a cotton rope tensing
then raveling into many frayed strands,

shining moments leftover gourds
strewn by the road after harvest.

But we forge ahead like physics,
until longing dissolves

the face, until systems
of measurement are obsolete

and we fix our eyes
on the vanishing point.

DONUT SHOP AT THE END OF THE WORLD

Inside the donut shop
at the end of the world
she fills the dishwasher rack
with scratched flatware
and ponders her life of food service,
these waterlogged devotions;
wants to believe her attention
to the arrangement of utensils
matters in the world, people
demand spotless spoons
to stir their Coffee Mate
into burnt coffee.
That old man out front is holy—
see the focused way he washes
that section of sidewalk, the way
he scours the cement under the seats
clean as driftwood on the shores of this
secondhand island.
She and her hangnails
shouldn't be surprised;
this is seminary for the streets:
wrinkled hands here in the water,
fingering utensils like rosaries,
the special of the day a miracle
seven days a week.

MUSTARD GREENS, INTERSTATE 580

With enough olive oil and lemon juice,
it was easy for her to overlook the occasional
woody stem and bitter tang of it:
roadside mustard, dandelion greens,
right there at the freeway's edge—
first a bag, then the entire trunk stuffed
full. She came to carry a knife in the glove box
to cut the juicy weeds of this new country,
while her husband laughed
at the provincial poverty of it all—
eating greens that had been simmering
in car fumes and animal piss. Yet
for her, hunger was not just a distant thought,
but a chemical memory in her muscles, her
jaws. And out here was a veritable *Sound of Music*,
the hills alive, nourishing the village she carried,
whispering *yes, we will feed you*. These are new
melodies of unyellowed mustard in early spring,
songs of fullness, love. The crunch underfoot as she scouts
the freshest bunch. The squeak of swaddling in clean
flour-sack towels. The drive back in the brown LeSabre,
shrugging off banana boat comments. Later, at home,
she washes up a sinkload of mustard greens,
boils them gently for an hour.
Everyone eats.

KODA FARMS, SOUTH DOS PALOS

Rice loves the pixilated hills,
the valley oak in the center
of every orchard, silos
quivering in the distance
cubic tons of highway grit
and thermal inversion
merging to a point
near Dos Palos, that whorl
of wanting, one valley south,
where inflorescence
dangles heavily in the paddies,
like a pendulous goodbye.
I've missed you like breath,
like kernels of truth.
Let's meet in the fields
and grasp at heads of rice
turning ochre in the husks
while our central nervous systems
vibrate and hum like idling harvesters
waiting for the fields to drain.

Elizabeth Coard_____

Elizabeth Coard is a pianist, poet, painter, and dancer. Many of her poems have been published in *Song of the San Joaquin, Penumbra, In Other Words,* and *Poet's Corner.* She teaches music and is the current President of the California Federation of Chaparral Poets, Inc.

"Originally from the East Coast, I left the year after my parents died. I lived in Mexico for a while, and then San Francisco which I had first visited in 1967. I was excited to be back in the Bay Area for a couple years, but a quirky turn of events brought me to Turlock. I was house sitting for a friend who suggested that I finish my college degree. As a single parent, it was easier in the Valley where rent was cheap, fresh food abundant, and there were no distractions. What a cultural void. My art professors and fellow artists inspired me and encouraged the countless hours of practice at the piano, on canvas, reading, writing, and dancing the blues away. I attended my first poetry slam, Slam on Rye, at the Prospect Theatre, put my name on the sign-up list, and made it to the 2nd round. Since then I've discovered many open mics and workshops and joined the Chaparral Poets in 2006. I was fortunate to have Sam Pierstorff edit some of my early poems, which set me on fire to write again."

ROADKILL

I'm not a fast talker,
but my mind can do
back flips
around the corner
at lightning speeds
when you start to
lie to me,
so you might want to
put on the brakes and
look both ways
first,
ask yourself
what the consequences are
if you go left
when you ought to be
going right.
Take a good look
at that blinking yellow
caution sign and
yield the right way,
because the oncoming traffic
behind that little white lie
you are racing to tell,
is the dividing line between us,
headlights
inching out into cross traffic,
ready—
to run you down.

A SMALL PINK & WHITE SOCK

In this maze of dirty laundry—
he just shrugs when I ask, as if
butter wouldn't melt in his mouth.
A tangled scene I've seen before,
so I pull the sheets and unmask.
Lies from a lifetime consummate
the truth of a sordid, toxic history.
The DNA and fibers twist, entwine
and wring out the unspoken truth
which no super-brand detergent
can un-stain, wash clean as new.

Deception is not biodegradable
or a renewable form of energy.
The agitators are working hard to
shake it loose, filter and separate
filthy lies from soft inner threads,
but so much has unraveled, seams,
lining torn apart beyond mending,
there is nothing to hang on the line,
nothing left, but false colors, to offer
a warm sun or gutsy autumn breeze.
Nothing, to iron out before sundown.

WILD, WILD WEST

Cowboys & Indians
wanna play?

I know a warrior dance
that'll shake my Dakotas
to pointed peaks

A black hat to silhouette
caliente skies,
you have boots to mount & ride

Shoot the stars, gunslinger
blast my smoke signals
rolling thunder on your thighs

My red-tipped Mohawk
trembles the ground
like a line of buffalo on the horizon

Whiskey colored chaps
chasing down fire
like spirit wind on an outlaw trail

C'mon, Cowboy!
Bury your gun
in Mohikan land

Can you hear my wild call,
jingle jangle—heads or tails?

Bruce Crawford

Bruce Crawford taught history and civics for over thirty years at Los Gatos High School and retired as Department Chair. He belongs to the San Joaquin Chapter of the Chaparral Poets and won two awards at their 2011 Convention. In 2005, he won first prize in the Scotts Valley Poets of the Valley Contest. His poetry has been published in *Poets of the San Joaquin Anthology, Poets Espresso, Verse of the Valley, Prize Winning Poems 2011 California Federation of Chaparral Poets,* and the *Student Anthology Los Gatos High School.*

"I was born in Modesto and graduated from Downey High in '56. I worked in fruit, groceries and paint, had some good teachers, played football, sang in the choir, and tried almost everything. My friends were mostly Steinbeck type characters, colored by The Depression, WWII, farming, and draggin' Tenth. Modesto was mostly hard work, fun and poor. But, we felt we were rich and very 'cool' in our clean and polished custom cars, parked at the drive-in, after taking our dates to the State Theater. The vibrant colors around us led to deep memories, lifelong friends, world travel and imprints that continually get meshed with 'whatever' to create a verse, image, or a strange new concoction. Like a good friend, writing has always hung onto me."

HIGHWAY ALMONDS

An almond seed rooted beside the highway,
now it's a fifteen foot mass of white blossoms,
beneath, mustard and radish abound, and
an iris blooms near outstanding daffodils.

Perhaps spring has mastered the recession,
it doesn't seem to care about unemployment,
foreclosures, the falling Dow or bank closures.
It'll rain again, but winter is on the way out!

The tangle of blatant voices still promote their waste,
but, I'm outside chewin' the fat and mowin',
breathin' the calm air, watchin' clouds disappear,
making way for refreshing almond blossoms.

BIG SUR THERMALS

Our Big Sur headland on the Pacific Rim
is not metered by the breaking waves,
or the surf crashing on the rocks,
but, by the constant and erratic wind.
It rolls in from the north,
ripples on the dunes.

We hiked the steep cattle trails.
At noon, we sit, face the wind
on the cliff's edge.
In the rocking kelp beds,
otter heads pop up.
Pelicans soar up the staircase.
Each layer of the northern thermal
is a step casting us higher and free,
as feathers rising, we join the powerful squalls.

The angled cliffs, battered, broken,
layered and lifted, shadow the coves and bay.
This ancient bed greets newly feathered swallows,
in a frenzy by their adobe nests.
Cows grazing, tending their calves
stand against the whole gale.
Below, on the narrow beach,
a fisherman teaches his young son
the rituals of manhood, fishing and
together—meet the encompassing thermals.

By the breakwater, near a dozen fancy cars,
colorful young men, on sailboards
dance and play on the surf,
tiny puppets on firm boards
brush the tops of rough white water.
Their sails keep them soaring,
in magic fully spirited kites
out of our deep and choppy cradle.

Tina Arnopole Driskill_____

Tina Arnopole Driskill is a Modesto native, a poet/journalist and an advocate for the arts and for peace and a sustainable environment. She is a member of the *Stanislaus Connections* editorial board and edits "A Gathering of Voices," the monthly's poetry page. A member of two poetry groups, The Licensed Fools and MeterMaids, she has been published in *Stanislaus Connections, Song of the San Joaquin*, and has been a selected poet for Modesto's Poet's Corner poetry contest.

"When I was a fourth grader at John Muir Elementary School in Modesto, I was privileged to be in the class of one of the world's finest teachers, Ms. Walters, who asked us all to write a poem. I was invited to read my poem next door in the other fourth grade class, which was the beginning of my interest in and awareness of poetry. Subsequently, poetry became a tool to unload my teenage angst, an ego-shrinking experience as a student in Phillip Levine's poetry writing class at Fresno State, and a neglected practice as a young parent. My interest was renewed when I joined a writing group in 1990. Currently, I see myself as a catalyst for creativity and sustainability, as I seek out, gather and encourage poetic, musical and environmental voices to share with the diverse population of this place I am proud to call home."

HOME WATERS

I am a daughter of the San Joaquin
   The Stanislaus and the Tuolumne
      I am a native born of transplants
         My watershed feeds the world

My roots taste the waters
    That nurture almonds and peaches
       Hydrate melons and nectarines
          Round the tomatoes red
             Elongate cucumbers and beans
             Rice fields rest in their liquid stillness

These are the flows of Valley Oak tableaus
    Pastures connect with riparian habitats
       Their banks house beaver and kit fox
          Egrets and Blue Herons peruse narrow shorelines
        Woodpeckers and Magpies chatter high above

Three Grande Dames
    These smooth flowing ladies of many thousand histories
         Chocolate brown and deep deep green
         They are the washes of the Mighty Sierra Nevadas

Robust and boisterous with melted spring thaw
      Turning lazy in the Valley summer heat
     Steadfastly coursing despite depleted Autumn
   Headwaters making way for new Winter rains and snows

These are the ladies who watched Estanislao's
      Vigilante guerrillas raid unholy captors
        Whose nearby boulders became
     The mortars for Autumn acorn harvests

These are the serpentine waterways
   We would bridge over

Dam and choke with gated communities

These are the majestic Stanislaus
The indolent Tuolumne
The river of the Valley San Joaquin

Gordon Durham

Gordon Durham is a charter member of the Poets of the San Joaquin, now living in a retirement center near his daughter in the Napa area after many years in Modesto. He is a former member of the *Song of the San Joaquin Quarterly* Editorial Board. His publishing credits include *Quercus Review, Modesto Poet's Corner,* and *Penumbra,* among others.

"I was part of the diverse group that Aileen Jaffa frequently invited to events in her home. My first mentor was my Aunt Genevieve Mott, who taught English at Santa Rosa Junior College. After attending Asilomar in 1984, I pursued creative writing, especially poetry, with various professors at MJC and beyond, beginning with Lee Nicholson, continuing with Lillian Vallee, Mara Fagin and Sam Pierstorff, and attending the Mendicino Coast Writers' conference. There is no certain time or place where I like to write, though the feeling tends to come in the evening. In settings near fountains, flowers, shade—it's easy to drift internally into the spot where I write. I write a few words and, if I'm lucky, the poem follows. I write because I have to. I can write my feelings better than I can speak them, wanting to create something and leave something behind when I'm gone."

FULL MOON SWIMMING

Her moistened smile from just below
the surface of my backyard pool
drew me out of the midnight air
and into her reflected glow.

Entangled there in bright morass—
refracted silvery beams that brush
the darkness of my submerged limbs
and lure their summer coat adrift—

we swam together through the night
until her reassembled form
climbed out along the western edge
and vanished over tiled horizons.

THE QUIET NIGHT LIES DOWN

The quiet night lies down
at the end of a hard-ridden day,
shunning all the thin gray shadows
to stretch on moonlit hay

among the field mice and owls
and lovers unaware
of all the deadly games at play
in innocent autumn air

while smooth gray mocking birds in tune
with spirits of the night
sing serenades to everyone
till just before daylight

when night arises with the sun,
accepts his lifting arm,
rides with him on his daily arc,
and lends the day her charm.

Pat Egenberger

Pat Egenberger's first published poems appeared in the early 1970's in *Original Works*, a multi-language poetry journal. Locally, *Song of the San Joaquin, Modesto Poets' Corner,* and *Between Sheets* have published various poems over the years. Other publications include *Spirit of the Rose Journal, Women Talking, Women Listening, and Medicine Jug.*

"I have benefited from vibrant local poetry groups as well as individuals. As co-director for the Bilingual Great Valley Writing Project, I had the pleasure of working with local poet Angela Salinas Morales, writing poems in Spanish and English. I have enjoyed Poetry Slam events, Tuesdays at the Barkin' Dog, and writing poetry in a literary naturalist workshop in upper Yosemite. I was fortunate to work several times as a co-presenter at Asilomar with local artist/poet/teacher James Shuman. For years, I participated in a writing group that included poetry and prose. As an English teacher I always incorporated poetry writing into the curriculum.

The flora, fauna, and vistas of the Valley, the foothills, and Sierras provide rich material for my poetry. I work as well with the life cycle, mundane tasks, spiritual questions, emotions, dreams, family, friends, strangers, Jungian themes, humor, and literary models— no subject too elevated or too modest."

JACK LONDON'S WOLF HOUSE

This house of light and laughter stands dark, silent
in its redwood crypt. Sonoma red rock
slowly feeds moss and lichen, cries broken
toothed to a placid sky. The vernal
reflection pool, a cement basin for
dry twigs; the servant's hallway, a rat's
racing course; the dining hall, an airy dream;
the fireplaces, strange totems or
obelisks; the empty rooms, eloquent
stories of the masons' art. Here a whimsy
of unplaned rock. There a massive boulder
bulging from the wall. This house grew from
wildness, from realistic imaginings.
Shreds of adventures and ideals hang
on its ramparts.

How could the house of a thousand years
snuff out like gauze in flame?

Poor man, rich man, socialist, scholar,
bon vivant, consummate host,
individualist, adventurer
still lives in a stone and charred redwood
monument in this Valley of the Moon.

I DO NOT WRITE LOVE POEMS

I wear the toga of my pain so well that
I clothe my sorrow in rarefied dignity, you say.
The gentle wrapping sequesters the rawness
of all those missing pieces where loss
consists of delicate incisions to each of my
innards, precisely slicing away the ganglious
nature of intimate connectedness.
It had to be removed because that is the
way of flesh. The living and the dead
can't share the same body anymore.
The ephemeral of memory may sound like a
balm to these gaping wounds, but that's for
Hallmark to say. I'll take my toga, thank you,
to hide what is mine only.

You can not know where the sutures are and
you do not sleep with seeping sounds where the
juice of my spirit leaks out at night. This
elegant robe is the shroud I wear for now,
night and day. Its threads will unravel some
day, but I will always don it as a sort of mist,
the exoskeleton of a woman whose contours
can never totally hide the places where the other
woman is missing.

VANESSA FERREL

Vanessa Ferrel grew up in Soledad, a small town south of the Salinas Valley, otherwise known as the salad bowl of California. She moved to Modesto 18 years ago when she gave birth to her son, Noe.

"Writing has been a crucial part of my development as a woman and as a mother. I have always maintained some sort of journal that I've used to strengthen ideas and reflect on perspectives throughout my life. My writing naturally transferred into the form of poetry in my teenage years, but within the last 10 years, I've begun using it as an instrument to help define my views on life, love, social conditions, racial inequities and religious perspectives. My hope is that my work will contribute to my legacy, encourage people to discover new ways to communicate, and serve as a voice for those who are often silent in our community."

DIA DE LOS MUERTOS

Today we remember over 400 of Juarez's
half buried women whose screams
scrape the night sky, bottomless cries
captured in destitute deserts
shattering into shards of silence

We honor those who died while on duty
from heat and thirst
while nurturing green fields

The men that live by the sword
domestic and foreign
noble or otherwise
who died in the name of freedom

We pray for *mi hermanito*
who didn't get to see his daughter
represent the brown-skinned Cinderellas
on the white man's pagan holiday
we wonder if there are taco trucks in the sky
and if there really is a heaven for a G

We give thanks for the *abuelitas*
who hand made each meal
rolled *masa* with arthritic hands
whose backyards flourished in ancient remedies
for flus, colds or infections

We remember Alberto Sepulveda
the 11-year-old boy who was shot in the back
obeying an officer's command to lay down
in his Modesto home on September 13, 2000
we pray for the trigger happy police officer
who was sworn to honor and protect...

We of the sun kissed people
honor our dead, as did the indigenous before us

Today we toast the dead
dance with the unknown...

IF HIS BODY WERE A BARRIO

If his body were a barrio
I'd lay naked in forgotten alleys
infamous for spit and sin

I'd whisper poetry
in between acute seconds of piercing silence
before the next burst of gunshots

I'd graffiti his name on my walls
and low ride bravely into the paradigm
of beautiful poverty

I'd be Iztaccihuatl on his lap
a reservoir of volcanic love
just waiting for the perfect moment
to erupt

I'd be subtle shine
on bondo painted El Caminos
a brown bagged bottle of forlorn memories
rinsed away by reasons
to stop collecting strikes
for the night

I'd be an ominous
one woman crusade
picketing beneath broken streetlights
chanting for change
and progression

I'd crawl inside every tattoo
placed inconspicuously on brown men
become every mother / daughter / lover
they carved in their flesh
love them bold and permanently

If his body were a barrio
I'd blow peace in each of the 4 directions
enable him to love himself
so he can love me back
without restraint

If his body were a barrio

Shawn Franco

Shawn Franco is a young writer and performance poet. His work has recently appeared in *Penumbra*, CSU Stanislaus' annual collection of writing and art. He's a 2009 individual world youth poetry slam champion. He plans to eventually tour colleges and universities performing his work and to one day develop into writing novels.

"Well, like anyone my age who was raised in Modesto, I'm burning to get out and move to a different and bigger city. But, to be 100% honest with myself, I'm starting to grow more appreciative of this town and have more pride in it. For the last few years, I've become more involved with the art scene—Off the Air shows, Slam on Rye, and the open mics at the Queen Bean, just to name a few. There's a great community here. We have plenty of talent and I'm actually glad to be a part of Modesto and its art and writing family."

REVERIE

To the ghost of my own self peace
who I'm constantly trying to catch,
I dreamed that there were artifacts
buried deep within your trails
and that if I traced the map painted
beneath your coded dialect,
I'd find reason to believe
in the sovereign benevolence you kept in your word,
in your ability to promise nothing would ever steal me
from the reverie you give off every time I get close.
I was golden beneath the arches of your most fragile steeples
with my throat full of homilies delivered in brass vocals.
I've chased your steps through exhausted bridges.
I've caught the glow of your image
in a swarm of Northern Lights,
I've watched swans float across your eyelids
while you sleep and I've pond-dived
endless times for you to see me in a midnight dream.
I'm just looking for an empty field to feel small inside,
and for you to sit quietly beside me.
So, hold me to the wind
so I can have the dust blown off
that's collecting in my calm demeanor.
Set me off in the trials to find faith
in places where I don't have any.
Remind me that there are saviors in the light of your eyes
so easy to forgive and forget the worst parts of me,
and that it's okay to love even the worst parts of me
in the way that you already do.

CLEO GRIFFITH_____

Cleo Griffith has been published in a variety of journals: *Iodine, Main Street Rag, Cider Press Review, Aurorean, Quercus Review, Furnace Review, Dirty Napkin*, and many others. She has received, among other awards, the 2004 Pegasus Grand Prize from the California Federation of Chaparral Poets and the Stanislaus Arts Council Excellence in Literary Arts Award in 2008. She is the chair of the editorial board of *Song of the San Joaquin*.

"My husband Tom and I moved to Salida in 2000. Retired, I reconnected with my poetic self and took pleasure in the wide-open spaces of the Valley. Almond orchards and farms brought back childhood memories of apple orchards and farms where I first lived. The incredible network of poets in the valley has astounded and inspired me. Through the poetry activities I have also met many artists of other techniques and again been amazed by the number and the quality of works. I joined poetry groups and found my competitive nature unleashed, entered contests with a variety of results including some really, really good ones. I absolutely revel in the connections I have in the Modesto area, am honored to be hanging out with some of the absolute best people— not only in talent but in personality, generosity, accessibility."

THE BOOK OF A THOUSAND SILENCES
—for Tom

We are witness to a thousand silences,
heir to a thousand breakings.
Our impending night has no phrase
in this new vocabulary,
the flavor of morning has no syllable.

Even in our embrace,
we remain an arms-length away from
translating these unexpected new pages
where there is no noun
where there is no need for one.
Each hour of liquid memory slips beyond
the dimension in which we speak
toward final silence.

PASSING, PASSING, PASSING BY

The muted grind of refrigerator motor
moves across the air to touch my mind.
Kids at the next-door preschool shriek
and bounce against the fence.
In every old familiar room a clock
calls the marked-off seconds.
        I think I've never heard
        the silence so intense.

The vases stand so still, so empty,
colors nearly harsh.
The screens upon the windows gather dust.
Passing, passing, passing by,
the cars whip, never stop.
        I think I've never seen
        the sky so full of rain.

The slight worn brass of doorknobs
which many times I've touched,
the weight of slender letters in my hand,
the slick warm glaze of coffee cup
against my cool soft lips.
        I think I've never felt
        such distant, sensual lack.

I think the taste of salt
        will be forever in my mouth.

THE LAST DREAM

Give up the last dream only
when the patina of copper
peels from the edge of the sun
and spirals down upon the forests,
when the pages of the book
crumple, crumble, dissemble
dusty,
mirrors show no light,
ceilings breathe in rhythm to the pewter moon,
floors are ribbons of brass
woven across a foundation of ocean.

Give up the last dream only
when it gives itself
the golden music that cannot be heard,
that can only be.

Give up the last dream only
when you are in the molten heart
of eternity.

IN THE HOUSE WITHOUT WALLS

At the end of the *journey without distance*
on the porch of the house without walls
hang the chimes,
sidewalks are paved with clouds,
garden blooms are poems.

The house without a roof
shelters a small, open daisy
on the window sill which holds itself
in a house without walls or roof.

In a house without doorways
thought curls in comfort,
sits side-by-side with justice
both wide-awake on a laughing chair.

In a house with only foundation
live the kittens of posterity
comfortable in young strong bodies
knowing eight more lives are theirs
and that love's journey
has no distance.

FORTUNE COOKIE
—for Tom

Years are like walls made of concrete and bubbles
sharp opaque and glass-clear fragile.
After all the sunrises on darkness
and sunsets on unbalanced horizons,
we're a couple, long-married,
curtains of determination layered thick
between inadequacies, lack of confidence;
hesitations hidden in hugs
and the past a night-train receding on velvet tracks,
leaving the smooth comfort,
the belief in the tiny words
on a 2-inch strip of paper:

He thinks as much of you as you think of him.

JENNIFER HAMILTON

Jennifer Hamilton's work has been published in local journals, *Collisions II* and *Collisions III*, as well as in a chapbook she co-authored entitled *Origami Ideas* and four editions of a creative writing journal she edited and sponsored, *Blackberry Winter*, and has had her poetry on display in galleries in upstate New York and Modesto. She's currently working on a full-length manuscript and is an instructor of English at Modesto Junior College.

"My connection to the Modesto area goes back as far as one's connection could. I was born in Modesto and raised in the nearby farming community of Hughson. Growing up in a family of musicians, I have always felt attracted to the inherent musicality of language, and being raised on a farm provided much opportunity for exploration of nature and her mysteries. Relentless chores taught me the work ethic needed to really *write*, for a germinating poem, much like a young garden, requires cultivation and attention. Whether writing about the old split oak behind the barn, the Pleiades, the smell of overripe peaches in late August, or what it feels like to bloom, I can identify a childhood experience that is significantly present in the poem."

DIGGING DEEPER

clods of soil story cling to shoots of the past
farmer, cultivator
she tugs and exposes
in medias res
a verse she didn't remember she knew:

the grit of labour
under early saturday sun
a shed on the farm
cows in cacophonous competition
bees orbit flowers
hum middle c
nature's muzak
a rake, a hoe in mid-swing
and rows upon rows of trees.

OLD BOOTS

Tough as old boots
caked in pasture mud
the kind that clumps
with grass bits

A rip and tear
slight poke where
irrigation water seeps
soaks cotton sock
prunes toes

A chipped red sole
where barbed wire
caught mid leap
hangs on the heel
tug-o-war with gravity

Tough old boots
experienced
ready
　　　...here.

DEPARTURE

—for Mom

i stayed until nature's first green
hoping time enough would pass…
that with winter's frost
your crystalline pain would melt
to be washed away
by spring rain.

but as I turn,
there you stand…
in your bee-loud glade,
aware only
that in spring
Grief is gold.

Lynn Hansen

Lynn M. Hansen is a biologist and poet who navigates comfortably between the left and right brain. She spends many enjoyable hours as a classroom volunteer teaching science to elementary students. Her poems have been published in *Quercus Review*, *hardpan*, *Song of the San Joaquin*, *Collision III*, *Brevities*, and *The Gathering: Ina Coolbrith Anthology*.

"Modesto might be regarded as a backwater Central Valley town with little to offer those living here. But this community has been an incubator for me where I, like other writers and artists, have found opportunity and subjects to explore. Having lived in this area for over 50 years, I am in love with the grasslands, vernal pools, almond orchards in bloom, Holstein cattle grazing in pastures, tule fog, farmers markets, warm summer evenings, the Tuolumne River, and yes even the pungent dairy aroma. This landscape and my eclectic family ground me, inform my images, stimulate reflection and nurture me as student, mom, wife, friend, teacher and poet. Immersed in Modesto's artistic crucible I continue to follow an early admonition by my admired colleague, Lee Nicholson: 'You have music in your voice, keep writing.'"

TWO SISTERS
—for Gail

You and I traveled together
in the same car.
We had different trips.
As a five-year old,
I watched the gas gauge.
when the needle moved
toward empty, I began to worry.
How far could we go?
Where was the next station?
What if the car stopped?

You, one year younger,
gazed out the window,
welcomed the stark landscape,
smiled at the horizon,
accepted the unfamiliar,
anticipated meeting new people.
Unthreatened by the journey
you said you felt safe with me.

I gazed out too,
through the rear-view mirror
or back window,
noticing loss.
I didn't know how to tell you
I was afraid.

MEMORABILIA

At her death, Grandma left
few personal items, nothing
anyone wanted, except
her Bible, now lost. I was not
there to empty the house,
hold her things, one last time.

Had I been there,
I would have felt her presence
slipped on the yellow calico apron
edged in blue piping, stained
with tomato juice and rooster blood,
buried my face in its folds, inhaling
the aroma of biscuits baking in her kitchen.
I would have worn her black straw Sabbath hat,
skin touching the soft inner band
darkened by sweat and oils carrying her scent.
My feet would have walked on colorful rugs
made from scraps, crocheted together
from cast off woolen skirts, shirts, pants.
I would have held up the long black
scraper she used like Cinderella, to clean
soot from the wood and coal-burning stove.

But, at age five,
long before her death, I chose
how I wanted to remember her.
As she sat on the bed, clipping
her gnarly, yellowed toenails,
I gathered them like sacred relics,
gently pressed them to me,
discards, made holy.

NANCY HASKETT

Nancy Haskett retired after 34 years of teaching at Roosevelt Jr. High in Modesto. For ten years, she was co-editor of the Modesto City Schools poetry anthology for all K-12 students. She has had winning poems in the city's Poet's Corner contest every year since 1988, and she has been a winner multiple times in the Jeannette Gould Maino contest. Her poems have been published in the *Blackwidows Web of Poetry*, and numerous times in *Song of the San Joaquin*. She has also been the featured poet in an edition of *Stanislaus Connections*.

"I moved to Modesto in 1974 to begin my teaching career. I must credit the City of Modesto, Parks and Recreation Department, for inspiring me to begin submitting my poetry to their annual Poet's Corner contest. Once my poems began to be selected as winners, I had the motivation I needed to write at least two good poems each year. Except for those poems that reflect on my childhood and pre-Modesto years, most of my writing continues to be based on daily life here in the Central Valley: orchards turned into housing tracts, the unexpected appearance of a hawk in our backyard redwood tree, making apricot jam on a hot summer day, vacations spent in nearby Yosemite, and of course the day-to-day routine as a teacher, mother, and grandmother."

WILLIAM

At eighteen months
my grandson has already learned
to be brave.
Grandpa says wait here
I'll be right back
and disappears into the garage—

alone
momentarily abandoned,
taking big gulps,
lower lip quivering,
but no tears,
he stands in the backyard
holding only a shovelful
of trust.

ROLLER SKATES

You could say I literally skated through the 1950s—
schoolday afternoons and weekends
spent circling the block,
no helmet, kneepads
or ipod headphones—
just the percussive sound of ball bearings
on cement sidewalk,
the hard staccato rhythm as I pounded
over the cracks,
coveting my friends' smooth, white leather shoe skates,
riding instead on last year's black oxfords
clamped tightly to the expandable frame and wheels,
striding
pushing
gliding
jarring,
the skate key on a cord around my neck,
its shape just right to fit the curl of my tongue
as I flew along
experiencing the hard
metallic taste
of total freedom

Lee Herrick

Lee Herrick is the author of *This Many Miles from Desire* and founding editor of *In the Grove*. His poems have appeared in *ZYZZYVA*, *The Bloomsbury Review*, and *Berkeley Poetry Review*, among others. He lives and teaches in Fresno, California.

"I learned to write and be creative in Modesto. The passionate teachers, tree-filled parks, and a public library I loved as a boy, where my mother would let me check out all the books I could carry—these served as a foundation that would take me to Modesto Junior College, where I fell in love with language and words. When I think of Modesto, I think of its teachers as the backbone, and I had the good fortune to learn from many of them at MJC, specifically Paul Neumann and Dan Onorato, who opened my eyes to the larger world and made me want to teach. From my mother, who is an artist in Modesto, I learned about color and precision; from my father, I learned what it means to work hard and give back. These are poetic tenets, as far as I am concerned. Born in Korea and adopted to the United States, I did not travel the typical route here, but I think of Modesto with love and apprecia-tion—its diversity, its hope and beauty, the teachers and parents, the poets and those class-rooms on College Avenue where my desire to write first bloomed."

FREEDOM

Logic suspends it for only so long, given fire,
given water. If we, you and I and them,
were more elemental and less of the mind,
you could imagine the problems—skin,
revealed for what it is, less than what we
aspire to, given angels, given sky.
Look. Start again. We have the open
architecture for such capacity, a new line,
a real shift, directing the gaze skyward. Do not
let the roof or the net keep you from it. Do not
let that voice that sounds like your voice keep you
from it. It is beyond that, outside of your body,
aloft and everywhere you are.

SALVATION

The blues is what mothers do not tell their sons,
in church or otherwise, how their bodies forgave
them when their spirits gave in, how you salvage love
by praying for something acoustic, something clean

and simple like the ideal room, one with a shelf
with your three favorite books and a photo
from your childhood, the one of you with the
big grin before you knew about the blues.

I wonder what songs my birth mother sang in
the five months she fed me before she left me
on the steps of a church in South Korea.
I wonder if they sounded like Sarah Chang's

quivering bow, that deep chant of a mother
saying goodbye to her son. Who can really say?
Sometimes all we have is the blues. The blues means
finding a song in the abandonment, one

you can sing in the middle of the night when
you remember that your Korean name, Kwang Soo
Lee, means bright light, something that can illuminate
or shine, like tears, little drops of liquefied God,

glistening down your brown face. I wonder
what songs my birth mother sings and if she sings
them for me, what stories her body might tell.
I have come to believe that the blues is the body's

salvation, a chorus of scars to remind you
that you are here, not where you feared you would be,
but here, flawed, angelic, and full of light.
I believe that the blues is the spirit's wreckage,

examined and damaged but whole again, more full
and prepared than it's ever been, quiet and still,
just as it was always meant to be.

GARDENING SECRETS OF THE DEAD

When the light pivots, hum—not so loud
the basil will know, but enough
to water it with your breath.
Gardening has nothing to do with names
like *lily* or *daisy*. It is about verbs like *uproot*,
traverse, hush. We can say it has aspects of memory
and prayer, but mostly it is about refraction and absence,
the dead long gone when the plant goes in. A part of the body.
Water and movement, attention and dirt.

       Once, I swam off the coast of Belize and pulled
seven local kids along in the shallow Caribbean,
their brown bodies in the blue water behind me,
the first one holding my left hand like a root,
the last one dangling his arm under the water
like a lavender twig or a flag in light wind.
A dead woman told me: Gardening,
simply, is laughing and swimming
a chorus of little brown miracles
in water so clear you can see yourself
and your own brown hands becoming clean.

ADOPTION MUSIC

I am learning to play the taiko, to feel
how leaves reappear in the trees with such ease.
One monk says this will teach me to hear
the variations of my name:
how my lover sighs it,
how a teacher grinded it out like a curse,
how your mother says it, drowning in a lake
before she leaves you. How it means somewhere
between mothers, not quite the rose
but not quite the roots. Like the woman
who finds you says, *Lee*, like a discovery—
one more child found in the world's history
of found children. How she said it like the echo
of one plucked e string, a clear pang of delight.

Linda Johnson

Linda Johnson is a Berkeley native and Modesto transplant. She holds an MA in English from CSU Stanislaus and an MM in Music from Holy Names University. She's been an adjunct professor in the Arts, Humanities and Communications Division of Modesto Junior College for over 25 years. She was active in Stanislaus County Poetry in Schools in the 1970s, and is a member of several local writing groups. Over the years, she's been published in a host of small literary magazines.

"Over the past forty years, Modesto has slowly revealed herself to me as a truly extraordinary fertile valley for poetry and creativity in general. Many communities offer an overexposure of cultural treasures and opportunities. Modesto's treasures are just as numerous, but are not as obvious. One must do a bit of digging and even defend our community of artists to those whose superior attitudes blind them to our beauty. Our strawberries, peaches, people, arts and tule fog offer abundance to those who will only see. Thank you, Modesto."

TO TOM AND SARAH

They bought the house when it was new.
Picture windowed and turquoise
Three bedrooms, one bath
Six thousand dollars cash

A sixty year old almond tree
Still spring blossoms in the side yard
Buzzing pink reminder of this
Fertile orchard land

They came from the bowl
That blew strong stock to California
Raised two sons, a daughter
Still live close, closer now that Tom's gone

Before he passed
They sang late into the night
A Hank Williams twang to those duets
Of sweet by and byes

Wind chimes fill her breezeway now
Gusts of gospel freely given.
They told her today there'd be no more chemotherapy
Nothing more but close the door

Keep her in this old house as long as possible
Listen to the new neighbors'
Baby cry late into the night
Rest easy now in the loving arms

Of Jesus
Sing "take me home oh lord, take me home"

THINGS WE JUST SAY

When I say, "Drive safely"
I mean, "May the road open clear before you
and may your path be a white light of confidence
piercing the dark."

When I say, "Call me when you get there"
I mean, "The fist in my gut of imagined terror
won't let go until you do. The forethought of grief suffocates—
I'm a diver with my tank on empty."

When I say, "Kiss me goodbye"
I mean, "Press your love to me like a brand,
a sign scarred in stone,
impervious to everything—
even your leaving."

LOUISE KANTRO

Louise Kantro is a teacher, poet, and prose writer whose work has appeared in an *Anthology of New England Poets, Quercus Review, Rattlesnake Press, Song of the San Joaquin, Brevities,* and others. Recently, Pudding House published her chapbook, *Dwellingplaces.*

"Born in the Midwest, I've also lived in Puerto Rico, San Diego, San Francisco, Louisiana, and now Modesto, where I've been a resident for almost thirty-five years. When the first of my two sons was a baby, I started to write poetry somewhat seriously. When my sons entered school, I became a high school teacher. (My plan is to retire next year.) In the past thirty years, I've actually focused on writing prose, even to the point of getting an MFA with an emphasis in short fiction, and I have achieved some success in publishing short fiction and nonfiction. My writing groups are both for poetry, though, and lately I've written more poetry than prose. When my mother moved to Modesto, she joined me in these poetry groups, and the result has been a deepening of my love of and commitment to writing poetry. I have definitely been impressed by the quality of the poetry—and kindness—of the community here and am pleased to be a part of it."

ELEVEN HOURS IN A TORNADO
ON THE WAY TO RENO

Like children lining up
at the classroom door, we sit
separated by glass and steel,
neighbors, the wave-at-you
but no-time-to-chat kind.
We peer out into a shiny dusk,
a gray that never becomes black
(not even at midnight),
watching tiny pearls float:
wondrous, mysterious, perfect.

Danger is here, too.
We can feel it.

Though each alone,
that we are many sustains us,
but more powerfully
night itself draws us close
to its chest
pats our backs
looks into our eyes.

When the line moves
ever so slowly (but it does move)
the Y of lights shows that just ahead
is a place to put chains on tires
or—oh, sweet relief—
to begin the return.

BIRDS TAKE TO THE SKY

They travel close,
a rope of bodies
that come to settle
horizontally on branches
or telephone wires.
Highly regarded for grace
when one bumps into
a third-story window or
plummets from a tree
we humans don't quite
know how to help a victim
of such terrible

gravity.

INGRID KERIOTIS

Ingrid Keriotis received her MFA in Creative Writing from Eastern Washington University. She teaches English at Modesto Junior College and raises two daughters (the source of much poetic inspiration). She has been previously published in such magazines as *Quercus Review*, *Song of the San Joaquin*, and *Alehouse*.

"My inspiration comes from my poetry students, some formerly addicted, others love-sick or broke, many who are secretly wondering if they are poets. 'Should I even be in this class?' one asked me—he went on to win awards. And my garden, even the bermuda grass (I must have something to wrestle besides my kids). They are three- and five-year-old girls who are so poetic in their syntax, as well as their thinking and ways of being. I can still hear Zoe yelling at the sky after days of rain, 'Sun, reach down with your long hands!' I am also thinking of Kay Ryan, Maya Angelou, Dorianne Laux, and all the other amazing writers who have come and spoken at Modesto Junior College, spreading inspiration like a good, hearty manure to fertilize us in need (which is us all)."

UNCIVILIZED

Just because I have a garden
I might become
uncivilized,
glad at the spiders and flies
entering through the open door

And if they don't?
I have no reminders of
the wildness we have undone
for armchairs and DVDs

My insides shake to plant, weed
but days of mail, piles of clothes
the clutter of the domestic
ensnares me

I am like those before me
who carried extra gunpowder for bears
but at least they slept outside like evening grass,
kissed with dirt on their lips

My fingernails
too clean
I am alarmed by
my lack of scent,
delicate feet squishy with softness

Busy modern fingers search drawers,
appeased sadly, momentarily
when grasping
the right pen.

LIGHT ON SKIN

What if you could string together
the best parts of
years, days, weeks?
I would leave out the ones I lost
when I didn't know
the president, the season, the backyard outside
my stained window.

The four o'clock sun hits
rows of almond
trees, deep blue clouds
drumbeats of machines
in a distant orchard
descend on the earth like footfalls.

No chemicals in the air today
the birds are taking deep breaths,
hungry cows face me in the austere light.

Past an abandoned barn I turn
for home
the yellow winter grass brushing my legs
I would never know I was ten minutes
from the city, those old
apartments like dirty shoes, the alleys
of broken glass, syringes
I would never know if I hadn't
reminded myself just now, wind in my fingers:
without addiction, I wake to life.

MAY FOR ZOE

I want to breathe in
the oaks by the river
as I did in the early days
before the bed rest,
when I would tell you about spring

how in California it comes
early, like the contractions
three months premature
your home pushing in on you,
the pressure
of each wave.

I imagine you emerging
into a world of daisies
and pollution,
almond orchards
and unending asphalt highways,
rivers and uncharted caves.

I stare for a moment
at the lines in my own long fingers
and recall the forgotten home
I left inside
my own mother—
the now quiet
place for me
she carries with her still.

SONGS

Soft as splinters pulled from blankets
offered like sweaty pennies from an opened palm
their crazy, annoying tunes
are like church music from a bad organ
and a half-vacant choir
when the priest
holding the holy book in his hands
gives less light than the winter sun through stained glass

I haven't said anything
I have nowhere to say it
no space or time
to fill
like freshly washed wine glasses
or stockings ready to hold the shape of gently curved toes

The din of children's voices creeps
over my ears like mites
repetitive, thin little songs
that keep me
from mine.

DANA KOSTER

Dana Koster received her MFA from Cornell University in 2007, and in 2008 was a finalist for both the Cultural Center of Cape Cod National Poetry Contest and the Iowa Award. In the fall of 2011, she will begin a Stegner Fellowship at Stanford University, where she intends to finish her first book of poems. Dana's work has appeared in *The Cincinnati Review, Bellevue Literary Review, Quercus Review, Berkeley Poetry Review,* and *Goblin Fruit,* among others.

"Though not a native Modestan myself, I will always love this city because it was the birthplace of my husband, Justin Souza (a poet also featured in this anthology), and our newborn son. Currently, the three of us make our home here with our lush vegetable garden, two cats and backyard chickens. In its own way, Modesto has given me the life, art, and daily inspiration that is my family."

KABLOOEY
Ghazal for America

The man on the TV says someone we love is always dying
but he's wrong—everyone we love is always dying

and what's more I tell him what's more is that miracle vial
you're searching for won't fix a goddamned thing. Diane

I tell him though that's not his name Diane no elixir will
grow back your ladyfriend's skin. It's kablooey. It was dynamite

back in the day but now it's something off the butcher's block
and I'm sorry darling but she's kaput. Times are dire

and if I lost a leg outside the green zone you'd tell me
the same thing. Maybe you're more a *diamond*

is half full sort of guy I don't know—I've never been
much of an optometrist. Chances are we won't be dining

this way again so I'd like to say before you sign off:
expletive deleted. You're a real pal a dynamo

in the sack but don't fool yourself. We're only watching
because those folks on the other channels are always dying

to sell us five-in-one pasta strainers and knives that cut through
tomatoes. But really don't all knives cut through tomatoes Diane?

OUR LADY OF THE UNVACUUMED FLOORS
Ghazal for my son

The doctor says six weeks til I unearth you, force
your skull past my broadening pelvis, the fiercest

struggle either of us has agreed to. So far you've
had it easy, kiddo, leeching iron and zinc from

my insides, snug against the beanbag of my bladder.
I want to complain, to remind myself of forlorn

weeks spent cursing the tartar sauce in the fridge, but
even when you knee the wind out of me I'm fiercely,

outlandishly composed. I, oh Lady of the
Unvacuumed Floors, have spent hours cataloguing four

dozen onesies, twenty two sleepers, thirteen hats.
Baby books call this nesting, but I know it as fear—

soon you'll be born of a disowned mother and an
unemployed father, into a world that's wholly fucked.

This is the safest I can keep you: lugged around
not like a purse but a new organ, abruptly formed.

PANTOUM: CHICKEN KEEPING FOR BEGINNERS

The chickens are nagging us from the backyard.
Having laid their daily eggs, they are disgruntled
by a lack of service. *You are too slow with the pellets,*
they cluck, and pace back & forth outside the window.

Having laid their daily eggs, they are disgruntled by
the rain that floods our yard and wets their feathers, so
they cluck and pace back & forth outside the window.
The garage slowly fills with water, puddles growing by the day.

The rain that floods our yard and wets their feathers, so
welcome after the summer drought, drags on for weeks.
The garage slowly fills with water, puddles growing by the day;
these flatlands were not built for such weather.

Welcome. After the summer drought dragged on, for weeks
there were harvest clouds billowing through the town.
These flatlands were not built for such weather,
but for containing the things we need, and nothing more.

There were no harvest clouds billowing through the town
the night our son was born, only fog and a convoy of Walmart trucks
built for containing the things we need, and nothing more.
Our son does not yet know to hate this place.

The night our son was born, only fog and a convoy of Walmart trucks
populated the road from our house to the hospital.
Our son does not yet know to hate this place.
The chickens are nagging us from the backyard.

Debee Loyd_____

Debee Loyd was the city of Modesto's third Poet Laureate from 2000 to 2004. She is currently a grandmother and has published many places, and nowhere at all. She has made many poet friends and some not so. She is taking the 2nd half of life to listen, take notes, chronicle.

"I am a poet, musician, grandmother—who handles hot potato life on valley floor juggling balancing on narrow beam between success and disaster observing others doing the same writing it down shouting for echo effect waiting."

JUNIPER FIELDS

toyota corolla lurches straight up from the red dirt
tires touch nothing while
buzz-cutting its way east through the wild
weeds

outside Oatman, Arizona
heaps of junk cars
millions abandoned
mouths open and tongue-less
thirsty

thousands of dreams dashed
dust under sandals, cowboy boots
clogs, high-heels
sneakers

i clutch my dreams in an amulet
hanging around my neck
bouncing between breasts
i did not leave a single dream or wish
in Oatman, AZ

i strapped them down
to keep them from blowing away accidentally
as i walk barefoot down the long hill

REMEMBRANCE OF CHILDHOOD

the slender stem solos
an acrobat
toward Jupiter

pushing through the acrid
nostril-stinging dirt
from the central valley
sand pounded to dust
baked at broiling
left to lie fallow

through the stench of dog pee
or growth hormone
nothing keeps the seedling
from becoming a flower

ARLENE SILVA MATTOS_____

Arlene Silva Mattos was born on a ranch near Turlock, grew up on a ranch near Riverbank, married and moved to a ranch between Empire and Waterford. She has written poetry and prose all her life and has received numerous awards and publications. From 1996 to 2000, she served as Poet Laureate of Modesto. While serving in that capacity, she visited schools throughout Stanislaus County, listened to poetry of the students and shared her poetry with those students.

"My connection to Modesto is important since I have lived in Stanislaus County all my life. Modesto is central to my life and my poetry reflects the flatland, the fertile fields, the irrigation from canals connected to dams, my farm background. The Valley produces fruits, nuts, vegetables and meat for the world. On hot nights, it is important to lie on a blanket under the stars and commune with the owls, mockingbirds, frogs, coyotes and other night creatures. On hot days, it is important to harvest the almonds, walnuts, peaches, apricots and myriad vegetables. I do not do

well in the Sierra Nevada Mountains where roads twist, rocks tumble onto trails, small animals skitter on hard ground, flowers work diligently to bloom for their short life. I live on the fertile flatland. That's much of what I write about and I love every bit of it."

SPIDERS

According to a filler
in the newspaper,
"spiders preceded dinosaurs."
Spiders were here before dinosaurs
and lived through that
awesome cataclysm which destroyed
all those gigantic brutes.
Spiders have continued
to spin wondrous
web patterns
these billions of years.
Therefore,
who am I
to dispatch spiders
from high corners
in my house?
They are surely
weaving the pattern
for us to follow
so we too may live through
awesome cataclysms.
These webs will save the world.
Weave on, I say!

WINDOWS

It is 7 A.M.
and I am washing windows.
Two Scrub Jays
in their blue dress-jackets
and matching gray shirts
hop across the lawn
and critique my work.
Mockingbirds measure my strokes.
A little pair of Linnets
raise a family
in the birdhouse.
They wash no windows!
A Great Blue Heron
flies silently, deliberately
across our clover.
I should never have seen him
but for his reflection
in the windows.
I stop my work altogether
and watch his slow grace
until he disappears in the distance.
The day begins to sparkle.

INDISCRETION

statue-still egret
awaits pollywog's slight move—
last indiscretion

Tom Myers

Tom Myers is a retired elementary teacher who has lived in the Central Valley most of his life. He lives in Modesto with his wife and pets. He has three daughters and two grandchildren living under the same western sky. His poems have appeared in *hardpan, Quercus, Rattlesnake Review, Collision II, Modesto Poets Contest,* and *Stanislaus Connections.* He has one chapbook: *The Lost Language of Birds.*

"I moved here in 1947 when I was six months old and Modesto was still a small agriculture community. I grew up in the 50s when one could ride a Schwinn to the city limits and beyond. The wild spaces within and surrounding Modesto are a part of who I am and the Valley landscape continues to provide inspiration for my poetry. Although I started late as a poet, I encouraged my students to write, share and publish their classroom poetry during my thirty-one years as an elementary teacher. Poetry provided them a safe avenue to express feelings and validate their experiences. For the past ten summers, I have been invited to teach a three-hour poetry session with students enrolled in the Young Writer's Workshop at Stanislaus State. I didn't begin writing poetry until the mid-eighties when I entered The Poets' Corner Contest. Close to ten years ago, I joined a local writing group, *awg,* of which I am still a member."

ANTICIPATION

The Owens River runs clear, scrub sage
and scraggily creosote dot the Eastern
Sierras desert.

Grasses tangle the current, submerged
algae sway like red and crimson tipped
porcupine quills. Congregations of speckled

rocks nest like killdeer eggs. A blue dragonfly
suns on a shallow snag, wings leaded glass.
She dips, skims water's surface, her dark twin

shadows the bottom. A fly fisherman stands
downstream: arm rides back, elbow and wrist
snap forward, rod stiffens then flexes, whips

back to front, fishing line arcs in slow motion,
a wisp of smoke, the caddis fly shudders,
just before kissing water's sweet lips,

> the way young lovers shiver,
> tremble with anticipation,
> as hands map unexplored lands.

UNDERCURRENT

Miguel drove his nephews to the river to
celebrate the end of school. Its smooth surface
deceptive like a siren's sweet song. The swift

undertow pulled them down, slender, young bodies
pushed along like blowing tumbleweeds. Today,
their mother wraps and unwraps the cloth around

her fingers, wishes she could wash away the pain.
She whispers the rosary, her eyes fix on the gold
framed photograph of her three sons on the

Formica table. Their father slumps forward,
head rests on his hands; dark sunken eyes
resist sleep. He looks up when the screen door

creaks, expects his sons to burst through playing
tag with cousins from Mexico. Doubt hangs heavy
in the kitchen like the plaster on the walls.

"I'm so sorry," Miguel mumbles. His tired words
evaporate. A brother whispers, "Wasn't your
fault. How could you have known?" They drift

apart like continents, conversations disconnect,
their timing off like a poorly rehearsed play and
awkward silences walk the room. Miguel grabs

another beer and heads out, walks slowly across
the backyard and stops where three bikes lean
against the wooden fence—lonely reminders

of the white coffins that rested side by side in
the church, where motionless, numb, he watched
the priest recite the funeral mass, saw his lips move,

but hearing nothing—remembers candles, the way
the flames danced and flickered, threads of precious
light bending, swaying, threatening to extinguish,

as if something were trying to blow them out.

Paul Neumann

Paul Neumann was born and raised on the coast of California. He has made his home in Modesto for the past forty-three years. He published widely in the seventies and then stopped for twenty years, although he continued to practice his craft. In 2003, his manuscript, "Forms of Light" was selected as the first book to be published by Quercus Review Press.

"I came to Modesto in 1968, when it was a city of some 47,000. Through my father-in-law, a local seedsman, I learned about the unique congruence of water, soil and sun here in the Valley. That lesson has never left me and has intensified as I have spent more and more of my time here. So now, in the twilight of my life, I am devoting much of my creative energy to making poems which celebrate what is present here—the life of the soil, the lives of the people who still try to make a living from the earth. At the same time, I have had to express my disgust about corporate farming, strip malls and the concretization of the farmland, as the small city I once knew has grown to a mega-sprawl of over 200,000. For forty some years I

have tried to read this land as well as an urban person can. I believe, deeply, that husbanding the earth is as close to God as we humans can get, and I only hope that my poems have made that idea clear."

AFTERNOON ON THE YAMPA

In the valley of the Yampa,
the wheat has been cut,
gathered into yellow wheels
and left on the shorn ground.
The harvester has been retired,
stands abandoned in the field,
and the time for work is done.

Fall is the season to settle,
before autumn turns winter
and trees lose their leaves,
time to gather the harvest,
store our fortunes, retire to
the safety of our burrows,
guard against the unexpected.

But here, on the Yampa,
a fisherman casts a fly while
the light drains from the day.
He casts again and again
in the face of darkness and death,
catching and releasing, never
tiring in the twilight of his life.

AGING

The light is fading in the west.
Only the highest branches of the pines
still hold the sun. We sit on the deck,
you and I, at peace in our chairs,
and watch the last brilliance of the day
begin to dim into shadowy night.

Can you feel the weight of these words,
the gravity pulling our sun toward
the horizon? But if summer were endless,
would we value this last light,
this glow in the tops of the trees,
the memory of this evening in the fall?

CALIFORNIA DREAMIN'

Walking up the yellow hills in twilight,
tawny grasses rippling at the road edge,
I move through the last part of the valley
left to itself and not brought to ruin.
A few cows browsing on the sloping hills,
birdsong drifting in a scatter of oak trees,
field mice foraging in the fading light.
And why have I come here? Where else to turn
in this muddled California fantasy but to
Del Puerto canyon? The hawk sails in a thermal;
The snake stalks the field mouse and strikes.

Below, the oven of a Central Valley summer,
heat rising off the asphalt, a stifling haze
that blurs I-5, McDonald's and the mega-station
where the drivers gas and use the rest room,
super-size a soda then hit the on-ramp.
They're hurrying toward the fantasy of Vegas,
the delusion of cruise ships or an air-conditioned
shopping mall, the intoxication of porn sites,
the drunken violence of a party crowd, the cruel
luxury of indolence and entitlement. Up here,
above Del Puerto, godlight rests with the hawk.

SAN FELIPE

After the wreckage of the marriage,
there was still a little money,
so I went alone to San Felipe,
to a small motel behind the beach,
ate prawns *al ajo* in a cheap cantina,
slept drunk each night on dirty sheets
and walked the morning sand, a nail
of tequila pulsing in my temples.
The Sea of Cortez stretched for miles,
empty ocean, empty sky, and I struggled
with the weight of failure.
                              When you fail
at what you once called love, your senses
turn to stone. You look out to the horizon
but cannot see the line between blue water
and blue sky; the order of the world is gone.
Across the Gulf of California, turtles swim
for miles to lay their eggs on beaches they
are destined for, and some do not survive.
But I was lucky. By chance I found a seashell
waiting in the sand, and in my ear I heard
the welcoming ocean.

THIS VALLEY
—for Bill

Through the valley's haze one sees
the smear of houses, the strip malls
clustered on the sides of 99, the mass
of traffic on the freeway, speeding
past this fertile earth, the soil and seed
now capped by concrete parking lots.
Small wonder that our children feed on
megaplex dreams, a feast of awesome
action heroes, serial killers and the casual
cruelty of ingenious machines, no wonder
that they seek miracles more complex
than the green weeds pushing through
small cracks in the sidewalk or the white
buds on the trees in the spring. Tilling the
earth, my Irish friend once said, is like
taking the sacrament, and when we work
the ground, turn the soil and ready the seed,
we slow our fall from grace.

CLAUDIA NEWCORN

Claudia Newcorn has been writing poetry since childhood, winning her first contest in 5th grade in Germany. She won two World of Poetry awards in 1986, and then her writing took her over into short stories and books, always with poetry woven in.

"Although born in the U.S., I grew up as a 'transfer kid,' moving 36 different times by the time I was 15, according to my mother's final count, as my family followed my father's job. My passion for writing started early in life. I wrote stories and poems from a young age, later becoming a reporter for Wellesley College's newspaper, where I earned my B.A. in English and psychology. I later graduated with an MBA from Northeastern University. In 1993, I launched my own marketing & communications consulting firm, Acorn Enterprises. My two award-winning books, *Crossover* and *Dark Fire, Krisalys Chronicles of Feyree* are soon to be joined by a third book to complete the trilogy. I write regularly for a variety of publications, serve as the editor for *Stanislaus Magazine,* and am a newspaper community columnist for *The Modesto Bee.* I collect fairy tale books, attempt to garden, am a certified holistic health care practitioner, and am passionate about hiking, animals, and the environment."

REVOLUTION #3

They farmed the lands
and tended crops
and sweltered in the sun.
      They next ducked smoke
      and drove big cars—
      briefcases on the run.

The crops are dying.
Smoke slowly thins—
or moves towards other shores.
      Revolution 3—
      at computer speeds
      has battered down our doors.

Mark Nicoll-Johnson_____

Mark Nicoll-Johnson has had poems published in *In the Grove, hardpan,* and *Stanislaus Connections,* and has read at the Mistlin Gallery—notably for the Modesto Art Museum's Surrealism Centennial Celebration—and at the Sacramento Poetry Center.

"I've seen myself as an exile here since moving to Modesto from Los Angeles in August, 1980. It's a useful trope. One of the first things that helped me to keep my sanity was Gerald Haslam and James Houston's anthology of Central Valley writing, and about the same time at a reading at CSC, Stanislaus (as it was then) I met the poets who would form the nucleus of the local California Poets in the Schools, among them my long time colleague, friend and motivator, Gordon Preston. I published a little chapbook, *3 x 3: Nine Poems from Los Angeles* in the early 80s, and for the next twenty years more or less most of my energies were consumed by family and teaching. Recently, I have been part of the last two Collision projects pairing poems with photographs and have collaborated with Gordon, Debee

Loyd and Tom Myers on a chapbook project to benefit the Mistlin Gallery. Like so many of us, I'm indebted to Gillian Wegener for her tireless work on behalf of local poetry."

SPRING SWELL

I smell bees and blossoms, my head swells,
Orchards become a haze of white,
Petals blow through supermarket parking lots,
Spring rises in spines to bloom in skulls.

Sunday I trimmed the mulberry tree,
And the fresh limbs wait now over
The alley fence for the municipal claw,
The mulch truck and the next phase
Of their strange story. I cut early

This year, and though the tree has
Not yet leafed, still tight buds tangled
On branches in the dust swell
In the warm light of our sudden spring.

ANOTHER SUNSET

Soon the leaves will fall from this shade tree. In
The cool my daughter plays on the tire swing.
From my arms a wide-eyed boy watches her
As I wait, peering west down the alley
Between trees, houses, fences, beyond the

Highway for the sunset. I think of you
A thousand miles north, a daughter in your arms,
Her eyes on noisy brothers all around,
Awaiting this same sunset, this same highway
Unfurling miles behind you. I recall

Another sunset. August, six years back,
We wound down through the Siskyous into
Oregon. The sky cleared after a squall.
Paired herons flew west. Red sky, road before
Us behind us. Where are the herons tonight?

Sam Pierstorff

Sam Pierstorff received his MFA in poetry from CSU Long Beach and went on to become the youngest Poet Laureate ever appointed in the state of California when he was selected to the position in 2004 by the city of Modesto where he currently teaches English at Modesto Junior College. He is the founding editor of *Quercus Review* and host of Modesto's monthly poetry slam, *Slam on Rye.* His debut poetry collection, *Growing Up in Someone Else's Shoes*, was published by World Parade Books in 2010.

"At 25, you don't turn down a full-time teaching position even if you haven't heard of the small town where the college resides. Suddenly, a dozen years later—a beautiful wife, a house, three awesome kids, amazing friends, great food, art, and music—small town life feels just right, and you don't ever plan to leave. I grew up in Los Angeles, reading Bukowski and swimming at the beach, and now I am 300+ miles north on Highway 99, gardening, teaching, coaching my daughter's tee-ball team, and writing when I can at one of the cool coffee shops in town. I run into people I know everywhere—on the streets, in stores, at a Modesto Nuts game—and I love the sense of belonging that comes with living here. It's hot in the summer and foggy in the winter, but the fruit ripens well on the trees, and great poetry grows here, too. I am blessed to be a part of our city's literary renaissance, blessed to be named as one of the Modesto Poets."

AND JUSTICE FOR ALL

You brake at the red light so hard
your briefcase slides off the vinyl
bench-seat of your rickety green pick-up
onto the floor, which you notice now
is stained with coffee, spiraled
in the shape of galaxies.

And before collecting the sharpened
pencils rolling beneath your shoes,
you sit for a moment, lean out the window
to breathe in the dusk of the Central Valley
where fog hangs loosely in the trees
like sheets of ripped muslin.

You never planned to be here
and you start to wonder what the hurry
has been all these years and why,
especially, you have never retired
Metallica's ...*And Justice For All* album
from the soundtrack of your life.
It's playing loudly even now,
at six o'clock in the morning.

Before the sun has bothered
to rear its orange head, you
have been banging yours
all the way down McHenry Avenue
just 30 minutes before you're scheduled
to teach a course in English Literature.

Men your age, you start to say
as you catch a glimpse of your paisley tie
and pressed shirt in the rearview,
*need to slow down, listen to Bach
or Benny Goodman, at least.*

And that's when sprinklers
on a nearby lawn erupt like wet fireworks.
You didn't think the spray could reach
across a whole lane of traffic,
but then you feel something land
on the back of your hand.

You look down at the bits of broken glass.
Could be water droplets, you think.
Could be goose bumps, too, rising
as the music in your truck swells
and your foot starts stomping on the gas
like it's a pedal on an old bass drum.

I DIDN'T KNOW THEY SOLD THAT AT THE FARMERS' MARKET

"When asked why they come [to Modesto, CA], prostitutes have told officers that they like the area. It's warm, so it's easy to be outside. And business is good, especially during the harvesting season." —"Nights on Ninth Street" by Emilie Raguso, *Modesto Bee*, 1/7/08.

When it's time for almonds to be shaken
off their trees, here come the hookers.

Lured by the warmth of Modesto's summer breeze,
they blow into town and shake the nuts from the twigs
and berries of men who stand for such things.

And I thought they came for the *Gallo Center for the Arts*
or the downtown restaurants, the sweet potato fries
at *Harvest Moon*, the Azteca Mocha at *Queen Bean*.

Why don't they come for art? Where are the garters
and fishnet stockings in the front row of the poetry slam?

If only they knew what poems could do for their body,
they would pay to stand under the hot water of our words,
and we could wash away the stains our neighbors left behind.

We are more than limp dicks in Ford pick up trucks,
more than sleazy motels and meth clouds rising
like ghosts from burial ashes.

But if they came to us, would we speak to them at all?
Would you play a song on your guitar or write a haiku:

>   *Lady of the night—*
>   *It's dark outside, so come in.*
>   *We'll take care of you.*

She'll tell you that "It's warm, so it's easy to be outside."

And for a moment, you believe her. But look closer:

Her arms are scarred as dead branches. Her face, bruised
and torn by the shears of fingernails and fists. Her mouth,
a dark well of missing teeth, you wonder if she even eats.

This does not look easy.

It's harvesting season once again in Modesto
when business is especially good.

So before the burning light of a new day dawns,
before you sow another wild oat, before you strip
your field down to its naked red dirt, ask yourself,

which hoe will you use today?

ON RESTRAINT

When my 2nd-grade son, who is studying rain forests,
points to the tip of South America on a world map,
which is drawn on the front of my T-shirt, and says,
"That's where an anaconda lives,"

it takes every ounce of maturity left in me
not to grab my crotch and say, "No son,
this is where an anaconda lives."

THE PULL

I spent the summer I was seven
in our neighbor's swimming pool,
mostly underwater so anyone
who looked down on me was blurred—
  their clothing, fuzzy rainbows,
  faces stretched like Silly Putty.

Nearly 30 years have passed,
and I am back in the pool,
this time learning lessons
my divorced parents never taught me,

  like how to stay on top
  of the water, in spite of it all,
  even when your ankles become anvils
  that want to drag you down,

  but still, as your body burns,
  you must reach out
  as far as you can
  with every stroke.

Watch now as my hand enters the water
the same way it slides into the sleeve
of a collared shirt, then *the pull.*

  The most important move happens
  underwater where no one can see.

Your wrist bends toward the bottom
of the pool. Your arm is an oar
  pushing the water back
before your hand snaps past the surface
  and circles back in.

And now, as I climb onto the starting block

and think about my next race,

I remember *the pull*—
how hard we must always push back
      if we want to move forward.

IT'S OKAY TO TALK TO STRANGERS

I remember the days when math books fell like leaves
from the sexy limbs of young ladies in high school hallways—

and if you were lucky, you'd be there to scoop it up
with the shovel of your hands and watch a smile
            bloom across her lips, a *Thank You* pour slowly
from her mouth like champagne into a wedding glass.

It was the 80's.
            Michael Jackson was walking on a moon called fame
and Prince was dancing in *Purple Rain*.

Instead of MySpace, we met at my locker
where real friends knew each other's combinations
and secrets were always safe inside.

We wrote love notes to perfect girls who never knew
how often they danced in the ballroom of our dreams.

These were *The Wonder Years*, when Winnie Cooper
splintered the hearts of every nerdy Jets fan

and high school strangers met in person
when they rubbed elbows in biology class
as they sliced open the stomachs of frogs.

These were the days before cell phones
when people had to talk to people . . .
and the best relationships were made
            by accident.

We didn't add friends, we made them.
And pornography
            was the *Snap-on Tools* calendar in dad's garage.

Nowadays, men type one-handed.
If they're not on their cell phones, they're jerking off.

So if a pretty girl drops her math book on the way to class,
no one is there to pick it up. But if a phone rings,
every idiot guy scrambles for his Motorola
as if he's been waiting his whole life for that call.

When will we pick up where we left off twenty years ago
when it took a second to say hello to a girl and a lifetime to forget her?

When will we hang up and listen to our hearts, close our laptops
and open our minds to the infinite possibilities of chance?

Look, while you were text-messaging your bonehead friend
about what a short little asshole your new English teacher is,
that cute brunette with emeralds for eyes just smiled at you
            and   you   totally   missed   it.

Tom Portwood

Tom Portwood is a freelance writer who works with non-profit healthcare clinics and other agencies. Having moved to Modesto in 2003, Portwood has been active with the *awg* writing group. A CD of several of his poems was produced in 2004 by *Zootsutti* Music, and he has appeared in *Modesto Poets' Corner*, *Stanislaus Connections*, and *hardpan*.

"While I have lived in Modesto for less than a decade, I think of the area as my home now, and love that almond orchards and grape fields are only a few blocks from our neighborhood. I love the cool autumn months and the deluge of falling leaves turned bright yellow or red, even the swirls of valley fog. Modesto has turned me into a better poet, too. I had been writing poems off and on since the late 1960s, mostly very unsatisfactorily. I was exceedingly lucky, then, to be invited to join *awg* within a few months of my arrival in Modesto. Through the highly constructive critiques and encouragement I received from all the fine poets in that group, I have learned much about the writing of poems. My approach to writing has grown more focused, purposeful during these years in Modesto. I have also been inspired by listening to the many accomplished poets who have shared their work at the Mistlin Gallery and the Barkin' Dog."

VITAL SIGNS

He arrived in the semi-private that afternoon
calculator, brief case
deals in the air
a hard, opaque smile.

I was in for tests that week—
the vital signs taken
and retaken
the blood drawn
and redrawn
the 24 hour E.E.G.

Toward dusk
his family clustered around the bed—
bright, nervous laughter
family jokes
a chat about grades with pimply-faced kids
a moment with the wife.

A little later
His docs came in—
the bespectacled family doctor
the heart man
the anesthesiologist.

I cannot say if
he was a good man
a failure
or a fool
or if he winced
at the suddenness
of gutted animals
on the road—

or if he had known

the treachery
of old allies at work.

But I awoke that night
and heard him talking softly
with his wife
of his regrets
and occasional resentments
of his love for her and the kids
his steady voice
cleaving the darkness
as I drifted off again.

In the morning he was gone.
I know nothing more
of the man.
Know only that we shared a room one night
and spoke a common tongue.

Linda Marie Prather

Linda Marie Prather is an editor for *Song of the San Joaquin.* She has two published chapbooks, *Painting With Words,* and *Pomegranate and Thistle.* Her work has appeared in *Penumbra, The Story Teller, City Works, Collision III,* among others. She has won honors and awards in numerous poetry competitions, and was nominated twice for a Pushcart Prize.

"After living in Texas, Arizona, and the Bay area, I was transplanted to the Central Valley 23 years ago. I have gotten to know and fallen in love with the landscape here. I had been journaling and writing some things of a spiritual nature, rather like devotionals, when poetry began appearing in these morning pages. I was delighted by this unexpected poetic visitation. Then one day at Thelma's Beauty Salon, where I worked as a hairdresser, I came across some work by Wilma Elizabeth McDaniel. Her voice was homey, entertaining, and somehow familiar. I had very little knowledge of poetry, but was smitten, and soon after, had the opportunity to hear her, and Lillian Vallee read at the State Theater. They inspired me to continue pursuing the craft. Many others in the community of writers in our area, through classes at MJC, guest poets, and workshops, informal gatherings at coffee houses, Barking Dog second Tuesdays, and poetry clubs have all continued to do the same."

DRY CREEK VIGNETTE

Just before sundown
there seems a million places to meander,
a bunch of stuff to gaze at, trip my artist bent—
so many compositions to invent.

Gold background, through cascading evergreens,
beyond to the walnut trees.
Gold on the barn's roof and side,
more on the white fence that follows the drive.

Down by the creek, the same still-life—
abandoned empty box of Camel Filters in the straw.
But, tonight, lying close by,
two soft feathers of the red-tailed hawk
and a small brown crumpled paper sack
adds new interest, charms me…imagine that.

Think I'll sketch it,
maybe come back in the morning with my art kit…
haven't the heart to lift it…that little vignette
that seems so peaceful.

DRY CREEK, JULY 26, 2009

I take the dirt path out where doodle bugs live—
powdery walk.
Bird claw and footprint,
      signature of dry places,
intaglio of the hardpan.

Tonight, no wind,
and I stand on a neat two-foot lane
firemen planned, scraped out…just in case.

Grass like match sticks under the oak.

Mauve shadows on the slopes,
birds in the thick July air
        doing their late day dance.

Big tawny cat stalks the hill, camouflaged
among the burnt stubble of summer,

sneaking up on feathered voices…trying
to see how close it can get,
      considers a chase….
then stops, like me, at contemplation.
…………………

Doves peck the ground up around my spot,
where a single sunflower blooms.

And the ants are back, big time, rummaging about
      in what remains of last spring's green.
Doesn't look much like itself
        and neither do we at sixty.

Ants run the length of scattered sticks—
      bridges to somewhere.

Hope one of them knows the way.
....

I shift, take the higher stance,
rest on the Dandl Orc 9 attachment.

A big roller of some kind,
something the tractor left behind in the space
          between the pepper trees,
where the road comes near the south fence.

Sun slipping away.
Birds stepping it down, readying for nightfall,
wringing out the last commentary,
          starting to let the quiet reign.

I came out here to lose the 'hood, dampen down
the daily grind of input-
the fall-out and stack-up of what occupies.

Think I'll drop off, get back in the dirt, see if
I can be like the insect,
look through the eyes of an ant,
                    hear with its tiny ears,
          with quick legs,
outrun the stuff, hone in on my purpose.

GORDON PRESTON

Gordon Preston has had poems in *Blue Mesa Review, Comstock Review, Cutbank, The Missouri Review, Rattle, Tary Wolf Review.* He was 54 when Finishing Line Press published his first chapbook, *Violins.* Now at 60, he still teaches reading and writing to the very young in Modesto, CA.

"After attending San Diego State, Colleen O'Brien and I arrived in Modesto in the autumn of 1977. I quickly fell into the local poetry scene that included the late Lee Nicholson. Another poet I met, and was tremendously influenced by, was the late Estelle Milligan, co-editor of the poetry quarterly *big MOON,* which called Modesto its home for some time. Also during that period, Bill O'Daly, co-founder of Copper Canyon Press, was living here and translating his first of eight volumes of Pablo Neruda's poetry. I was busy publishing the last two issues of a poetry magazine titled *Cafeteria.* I later hosted a monthly poetry reading at the Mistlin Art Gallery in downtown Modesto and found support and friendship with fellow poets, and many writing groups such as the glorious The Licensed Fools and the Chaparral Poets. I was an editor with Debee Loyd and Karen Baker of the poetry journal *hardpan,* which lasted a life long enough to connect a Great Central Valley community of writers to one another in a neighborly and meaningful manner."

FIRST GARDEN

What to say
about restless sleep
and weeds that disturb the garden.

I hoe them in the brown heaven
we share under our bare feet.

I look at you, bending there

a heart, and a soul, and a dry wind
slowly rise to delight the sky.

HOLIDAY WEEKEND

The sun and music drove us to the pool,
crowded pool, much like river animals we were
complete with cups, colorful beverages floating in air.

River animals move slow, half standing,
half floating, sporting sunglasses, hat maybe,
nude marine statues lapping in the chlorine tide.

Random bodies gather, vegetables
floating in a bowl upon a lawn, sandals
abandoned on the deck, household keys lost

in beach bags as well-behaved children played
in the deeper end of life. First names became familiar
as the city-towns along the north/south Hwy 99. All-American

as rainbow trout, salmon headed up-streams
past green canvas tents with clotheslines a banner
of white socks absorbing light and wind like hearts

and feathers released from a cage. The brave moon,
in the middle of everything, is the last candle blown out.
And the plans of lovers and ships tie knots at the water's edge.

MOONLIGHT

is a straw hat
resting on your lap

an autumn evening
where the willow

is a green brass temple
silently fishing in the air

and someone gay
holds up a plum

to halo the horizon moon
against a darkening sky.

Later, the stars join in
brushing at our window

with wings of green leaves
shadowing upon the waters

that float all the saints blessing
each stone of our Earth.

PASSENGERS PASSING THROUGH OUR LIVES, SFO TO CANCUN, 12/29/10

The air terminal crowds, one
Walks like a bird, looks into the glass
Searching for other egrets.

Another with a cane, flat handle,
Professional like a preacher,
Could have the voice of a mountain.
Fire in his mind, forbidden to love.

The pregnant one, alone.
Compass resisting authority.

One a bookmark, advancing antiques,
Perhaps for a very last time.

A ballerina without slippers, walking
Into a storm, covers her shoulders, bare.

Someone unisex, irreversible.

A couple married one too many years,
Syllables breathing their indifference.

A mother with daughter like
A canoe tethered
To the lake landing.

There is black & white before dawn,
One walking like a bowl of water,
Dipping into space, into a foreign lan-
guage.

Boarding passes, ticket stubs,
Dead Sea Scrolls.

Little babies, little moons
On the carpeted tram-way,
Voices calling like candle-lights.

Red hair, black hair
Electronics in hand.

Silent fathers, stoic sons,
Terminal cancer of age,
And stars fade above the horizon.

THE HORSE RANCH
—for Pam Eau Clair

Is hope
the hard wood
heart of a tree....
Is it among
the horses
you brush down
after the morning ride
when children dance
in the cookie dough
mud of the meadow...
Have we learned
the unpaved road
to age is slender
as the pianist's hands...
And the young aspen
at the edge over there
is ivory as teeth
or saddle soap
upon the jaws of leather...
We both longed for work
the barn door opened for us,
those ordinary wooden ways
of gloves gripping rope,
straw strewn about with dust,
its golden hair fallen from rafters
reflecting warmth and memory,
of feet bare in thin yellow light
slipping through brown cedar planks
onto a dirt floor all alone each evening.
With age, our hearts are bound
to all of this, giving direction
to the solid and to the beautiful.

KRIS PRICE

Kris Price's work has appeared in *BlackCatPoems.com* and *Penumbra*. He was awarded second place at Modesto Junior College in Kay Ryan's Community College Poetry Project contest, which she held during her term as the United States Poet Laureate.

"I currently go to Modesto Junior College where I study film and literature. I was an assistant editor for the *Quercus Review*. I'm a frequent attendee of the Modesto Poetry Slam, Slam on Rye, and the Barkin' Dog Grill's Second Tuesday Poetry Readings. I have also created a local literary journal called *Snail Mail Review*. I have been in Modesto all my life. I enjoy the area and its natural landscape. I come from a long line of farmers, and many of my uncles contribute to the thriving agricultural economy here in the Central Valley. My influences come from all around. Anything from a television show, a song, or my day-to-day life can inspire a poem. Writing is my passion, and I want to make sure that it cannot only educate but influence others to want to write as well. Through my writing, I hope to inspire people to change themselves and even possibly the world."

ANOTHER TOXIC RELATIONSHIP

Here comes the beast that lays the golden egg,
a night of zombie insomnia,
the clock singing the time.

Here comes a rat with a flute,
a hyena wearing drag,
a bat with a head of moss,
an old fart blowing fumes,
a fish sizzling in the sun.

Here comes a woman
wearing a halo,
a bullet,
a corpse bride.
Here comes a tiny fairy.
Here comes Juliet.
Here come the prostitutes.

All of them line up and form
a straight path,
a very long path.
The longest toxic path
you have ever seen.

BRENDA ROBERT

Brenda Robert's first writing attempts were short plays which she coerced her family into performing. Her poems have been published in *Touchstone* and *Kansas Quarterly*. Her PhD dissertation studied the life stories of women with disabilities, and she is currently working on her own memoir. Retired from a career spent teaching English and working in higher ed administration in Maryland, Minnesota, and California, she considers her years as Dean of Literature and Languages at Modesto Junior College (a.k.a. "Mother of Lit and Lang") as among her most memorable.

"Growing up among storytellers and living in small towns in rural Kansas shaped me into what I have become. My grandfather told me tall tales about coyotes and sheep; my uncles enlivened every gathering with their stories; and my father recited his favorite poems to his daughters. I've felt a strong connection to the past and to the land and to the lives of those pioneers. I once made a pilgrimage to the plains of western Kansas to see the lonely spot where my grandmother was born in a sod house. A collection of poems I'm working on about these places and people, 'Family Album,' will be for my children and grandchildren. I've come late to the serious writing of poetry, but I feel that perhaps it is only because the time is now right for the contemplation and dedication required."

FOG

Old Carl said the fog comes
on little cat feet.
But that's Illinois fog.
Modesto fog drops from the sky
like a crouched mountain lion.
Landing on your chest,
it sits there and suffocates.

Afternoon air is sweet and sunny.
Night comes with its sprinkle of stars.
But morning—oh, morning.
I peek into the mist to see the trees
blanketed by the gray that surrounds them.
No swishes, no flicking cat's tail
as it sits on silent haunches.

This fog hangs heavy.
Cars creep tentatively,
morning walkers appear from the miasma,
quietly disappearing once more.
I hear a scrub jay squawking,
maybe a corporeal cat lurks, lingers,
licking its paws and waiting.

We are all waiting.

NIGHT WALK

We walk through the forest at dusk
when the setting sun droops in the sky.
Light enough still shows us the trail.
Pine needles hang in clusters over
fallen cones that carpet the understory,
singly and in bunches.
Something small scurries across our path,
a chipmunk with tail erect like a flag to greet or warn.
A twig snaps underfoot, breaking the quiet.
A night bird erupts in a cloud of feathers
from a branch ahead, a small owl perhaps
disturbed by our presence.
Darkness closes on us slowly and the silence
breathes a heady green yet dusty scent.
Ahead darkened trees and trail converge until
nothing can be seen or felt.
We exhale our own breath and take in forest
scents until we are united in this act of
respiration, our own selves disappearing
and merging into the shadowy green.

George Rogers

George Rogers was a dedicated teacher who taught thirty years at Orville Wright Elementary School. His poems have appeared in *Quercus Review, Penumbra, Modesto Poets' Corner Contest* and *Stanislaus Connections*. His chapbook, *About to Fly*, was published posthumously.

"George made headlines the day he was born on January 24, 1948. He was proclaimed the 'Gold Rush Baby' for Stanislaus County. He was a valley boy who loved Modesto. He sang, played the flute and wrote song lyrics as a member of the local band, Wooden Nickel. George's poetry celebrated what he knew and loved: his family, friends, music, relationships and the simple joys of daily life. He helped produce a series of poetry events at the State Theatre and was a member of two local poetry groups, Licensed Fools and awg. His work was published in the inaugural edition of *Quercus Review* and he was the first poet featured in 'A Gathering of Voices,' the monthly column in *Stanislaus Connections*. George wrote prodigiously in the last years of his life, even up to the day he died. He will always be remembered for his wild sense of humor. A sharp wit and spontaneity were his trademarks. He was truly one of a kind. His passion for life was fueled from within, and his flame lives on in those of us who were lucky enough to know him."

CLAUDIA

I read Claudia's story
about her Uncle Rafael
shot to death when she was five
her grandmother telling her
everything is all right
"as if I was dumb"
she writes

I look at her the next day
smiling her smile that says
I am proud being
so knowing so young
writing myself inside-out
read me before I'm gone

EMPTYING THE BARN

What would we find
under the straw and dust
and neglect of those years
suspended in the loft
we hid in growing up?

It could be the postcards
your father sent you from
the ports around the world
or the bracelet I gave you
to make up for the loss.

It might be the photo
of my mother I ripped
into a hundred pieces
or the shoes I left
behind the day she died.

I am certain in this belief:
emptying the barn together
our bones will rise inside us
and we will stand clothed
in the clean skin of our souls.

RECESSION

The photograph seems like
a stranger's memory—
the young man
holding the baby over the fence
for the young woman
only the baby
taking anything for granted
squinting into the sun—
no shadows in the scene
everything stopped bright in time.

I look up
remember how quickly
the earth turns
the vision changes
the sun pushing on our backs
receding across the field
shadows growing among us
quickening us into the
falling dark.

Salvatore Salerno

Salvatore Salerno has an MFA from U.N.C. Greensboro, where he was awarded The Academy of American Poets University Prize in 1985. He was employed as a poet and playwright in the North Carolina Visiting Artist Program. Four of his six plays have been produced. More than 100 of his poems and short stories have been published in magazines, including *Quercus Review, Poem, Descant, Ohio Journal,* and *The Greensboro Review.* His self-published book is *Sunleaf.*

"I arrived in Modesto in 1987 to teach drama and English as a fading language at Davis High School. I wrote virtually no poetry from 1985 to 2008, when I was visited by a muse called retirement. Of the phases in a poet's career, I've been a rising star and setting sun, without the intervening noonday blaze of acclaim. I've discovered that there are ample opportunities throughout Modesto to be connected to audiences and other poets through readings at The Barkin' Dog Grill, poetry slams at the State and Prospect Theaters, the Two Roads interviews of local artists, and readings from the *Song of the San Joaquin* anthologies. Modesto is a city modest enough for us to practice that uncommon virtue, thereby tempering the strange wilderness of our art."

THE SCHEHERAZADE GENE

However else we must survive,
Whatever is kept or lost,
We also hunt and gather stories.

Our days, ludicrous or pained,
Trigger that instinctual thought—
This could make an anecdote.

We embellish by our natures;
The cold meat stew of facts
Needs flame and the spice of fiction.

Storytelling, neither food nor drink
Nor shelter, evolves into more
Than what our primal needs are for:

Like that Persian queen of wits
Who pleased a harsh king,
We spin our tales to stay alive.

Angela Morales Salinas

Angela Morales Salinas teaches kindergarten for love and money and writes poetry for love alone. She has been published locally in *Penumbra, Something So Write, Stanislaus Connections,* and *hardpan.* Currently, she is trying to figure out the business of aging gracefully.

"I came to this country speaking nothing but Spanish. When I went to school, I quickly learned to speak English. I fell in love with how two languages could work together to create something unique. I have been in the San Joaquin Valley for most of my life, starting at the very southern end, Kern County, and making my way slowly but surely up north. I have chosen to work in a neighborhood that many people do not like to think about. I understand. It is hard to look at want and fear because if you are not careful that is all you will see. You have to be able to look past that and see the absolute joy and hope that is there beneath the surface. This crazy mix of languages, people, and ideas has been my inspiration. There is beauty in the ugliness, and harshness masks a gentleness that's also there. If I can give voice to what our valley is trying to tell us, I will have done I think, what I was sent to do. But to accomplish this I know I must listen carefully, look deeply and allow love to guide my voice."

CALIFORNIA LOVE SONG

I know that you don't love me back
you don't care for
> the way I look
> the way I talk

the total disregard I have for arbitrary walls
and fences built to keep me out
> except,

you look the other way
when you need a gardener maid nanny janitor cook
someone to pick the fruit
> strawberries-peaches-grapes
> that fill your clean white plates

someone to plant, harvest, sew
cool cotton for your clothes
> someone who doesn't balk
> at the taste of blood or sweat

I fit the bill and yet
I know that you don't love me back
> My music on the radio is a nuisance as you scan
> For a country, jazz, Christian or alternative rock station,

It's worse than static-noise
> But then you'll catch a word
> A phrase you understand

Los Angeles
Merced
Sacramento
Modesto
Hasta la vista baby
> and even your own name
> the one I gave to you

California...
California sings her song to all those who care to listen
> of how long I have been here

how long I've loved your valleys
> your mountains and your rivers

your deserts I have tilled, irrigated
and filled with homes and children
the children that you hate
because their skin betrays them

and even then I stay
I teach, I doctor, I lawyer
I dance and sing, plant flowers
Grow corn, chiles, tomatoes
Bury my dead and pray
That someday, California
someday you'll love me back

SNOW IN THE SAN JOAQUIN

This winter,
      I anticipated snow.
It was so cold
      and lord knows
            we had precipitation
      levees broke,
          rivers overflowed,
               their banks could not contain them.

I waited.
But the cold,
      unable to hang in there,
         gave way to early spring
And almost in no time it seemed
      the almond orchards bloomed.
The trees lined up in perfect rows
Catholic girls in first communion clothes.

Now, they've begun to drop their petals
      in blankets of white
         row upon row
the breeze plucks them from their branches
      and they float
silent and sure
      as San Joaquin snow.

THREE LITTLE PIGS

One Sister built her house of bricks
    one by one she placed them
        in the mortar she mixed special
          strong
    and for good measure
        she cemented the foundation
It's a fine house, sturdy
        To get inside you have to knock
          All of her doors and her windows lock.

My other sister didn't care
    took only what was lying there
        She threw some straw up in the air
        and where it landed
          she called home
        She burns her walls in winter
          to keep warm
        When summer comes
          she dances with the wolf
            who would be at her door
        if her house had one.

Now Me,
    I built my house of sticks
    I am unwilling to commit
        to the one extreme of wild exhilaration, fear
        or to the other of solid permanence
          of habit
    I have doors but they don't lock
        still, I always check my windows
          when I hear someone knock.

Linda Gordon Sawyer

Linda Gordon Sawyer's work has appeared in the *Modesto Bee, Watercolor Magazine, Blue Unicorn,* and *Song of the San Joaquin.* She also illustrated a chapbook of her poems, *Leaf by Leaf.* She has four sons and nine grandchildren. She lives with her husband Tom, and dog Sophie on their ranch east of Waterford.

"I grew up in Berkeley surrounded by artists and writers. When I went off to UC Davis to study art, I never expected to find myself 22 miles from the nearest city on a very large ranch with hundreds of acres of walnut trees and lots of black and white cows. The Tuolumne River bisects our ranch, and when the disastrous flood on the river hit us in 1997, the waters destroyed our bridge to the rest of the world. I began writing essays about ranch life. Often those written experiences became distilled into poems. I began really thinking about what it meant to be living in the wide-open landscape, being subject to the whims of nature. I appreciated those who came before us: those who settled the land, the mule skinners who got up before dawn to hitch 40 mules to the combine harvester, and the women who served a main meal to 20 hungry men every day. When I finally joined a poetry group, I had a wealth of ideas for poems. It has been a wonderful experience to hear their work, and share mine."

RULES OF THE GAME

Begin at the sidewalk
where the pine trees dip to the ground.
Take time to smell the piney air
inside this cave-like place.
No one can find you.
Step carefully onto the fence.
Never touch earth
until the game is over,
or you are out.
Crawl to the Young's cherry tree.
Cherries hang in twos
and threes. Eat 'til you are full.
Continue to Mrs. Sloss's window.
She will give a scowl, knowing
you are up to no good.

Make your way to the next block
without touching down.
There will be a dog or two
and a broken gate in brambly weeds. Next,
climb the Doyle's giant redwood,
the tallest tree in town.
If you can make it to the top,
the wind will give you a ride,
and you can see forever.
After the climb, get back
by way of the Winstead's roof.
Shimmy down the banister
to the walk where you began.
10 points if you don't get caught.

LINDA SCHELLER

Linda Scheller is a teacher, poet, and playwright. Her work has appeared in *Notre Dame Review, The Ledge, Hawaii Pacific Review, The Distillery,* and *Poetry East,* among others. She has two children and lives with many animals, birds, and plants, both domesticated and wild.

"Thirty-five years ago, I left the Adirondack Mountains of New York and came here to California. I thought I would die. The Central Valley is the antithesis of the Adirondacks, and the heat and glare of the sun at first rendered me prostrate. When I discovered co-rec soccer and a thriving community of writers, I recovered and began to thrive. Circumstances, fate and naïveté had led me to Modesto and then Turlock, and after a brief but wretched stint of poverty, I decided to finish my bachelor of arts degree at Stanislaus State and later took the NTE and requisite teacher preparation coursework, thinking I could give the unlikely and undesired field of teaching a try just so I might earn a living. To my great surprise, I found a home in the classroom and a calling in the evangelism of learning. The

diverse world cultures in our valley population and the complexities of agriculture fascinate me. My writing has been informed by all these influences and experiences, and a rugged beauty is discernible in the landscape, people, and life of the Central Valley."

FARM WIFE

The roosters feel the sun approach
and call, hauling it up on a string of screams.
I wash my face with prayers, make coffee for the men
and cast pans on iron spiders. The baby cries,
the children punch away their dreams. New light
falls through gingham. There are cows to milk
and fields to harrow. The men depart in mud-flecked
boots and denim soft and blue as April. Backpacks
stuffed with books and lunches yank outdoors.
The bus swoops in, steel oriole, whisking
my children off to a pantomime of choice.
Dirty dishes, clothing wait like sinners for
confession. Bills, receipts and checks sift
off to cyber files. I feed the baby, vacuum,
pare vegetables, fold laundry and mend.
At noon the men return to eat and leave,
trailing sweat and hay. The dogs flop down
panting on the porch. I clear the table,
sweep, dump garbage, wash windows,
swat flies, drown ants. The baby naps.
I go out back and catch a chicken by the neck,
break its head off, drain and pluck our dinner.
I hear the bus roar back and set the children free.
Their voices bloom in the air behind me. Sunset
filters through the barn; tractors beetle back and forth.
I gather up the pans of blood and feathers,
send out the dogs, nod to the orchard.

MAGPIE

Cirrus white against glossy black
with rainbow overlay
like oil on the puddles of childhood

the magpie flies, tail fluttering,
shimmering in a trembling vortex,
a cyclone pulled toward heaven

streaking across the blue
oblique to earth, silent
and fleeting as dream.

Flat, dry and treeless, the valley
is a gallery of predators
stalking, waiting, striking.

Lizards trickle down rocks
flickering gray in the sunlight,
an afterthought of heat.

Coyotes lope through alfalfa,
tousled shadows of morning
gleaning the harvest of mice.

A tall, crooked figure looms silver
in the fields: a great blue heron
aims at some small, unsuspecting prey.

In a cloud of feathers
the magpie falls to earth,
beak agape, wings splayed.

The boy stands at the orchard's edge,
smiling with narrowed eyes
as he lowers the gun.

Tonight he will dream of flying:
a kestrel, soaring above the valley
searching for something to kill.

THE SKY COMPELS ME

Today, the clouds are so large,
First white, then silvering,
That I have to run inside
And tell my computer
How I feel

Between weeding and planting
A space appears to widen
The realm of possibilities

Between rainstorms and sunlight
The sky appears to signal
The change in mind

The floods have left me
Alone for now, and anything
I plant grows madly,
Waving red leaves,
Whispering

WEATHERED

Wind and children,
wet paint, flight of birds.
Hills ferry the dead
to the sea.
In my dream
I leaned against your back;
now I sit against stone.
Granite, I believe,
mica, feldspar and quartz;
prime numbers, justice, snakes.
You swerved for some reason
we will never know,
becoming a rocket without mice,
the perfect ellipse, an arrow.
Now the clouds
arrange themselves,
a chorus against a blue drop.
Nearby, a family of ten
sits around a grave
as if at table,
giving thanks.

JAMES SHUMAN

James Shuman is past president of the California Federation of Chaparral Poets, Inc. and past president of the Poets of the San Joaquin. He is on the Editorial Board of *Song of the San Joaquin*. He was a founding member and the first secretary of The Poets of the San Joaquin, and has also been a member of The Poets' Corner Committee of Modesto since its organization in 1982. He has been published in *Song of the San Joaquin* as well as *The Sentinel* (predecessor of *Penumbra*) and others.

"I have lived in Modesto since 1963, and certainly consider it my home. But I was born and grew up in Indiana. I won the State Poetry Contest in both my sophomore and junior years of high school, and was included in *Who's Who Among American High School Poets* in my junior and senior years. Upon coming to Modesto, I took classes at MJC with Gary Phillips and Lee Nicholson and was part of Aileen Jaffa's circle of poetry lovers. I served as a workshop presenter on poetry writing at the Asilomar conference for English teachers (CCCTE) for 2003-2008 conferences. The western landscape has been a big part of my background information, but I am also fascinated with how people interact with each other. Much of my recent poetry has been observation-based, sometimes the environment, but often the people. I also have enjoyed telling the stories of my ancestors and other people I have known from the past through poetry."

FROST AND FOG

Bright sun, clear sky, cold wind;
I turn my collar up around my ears.
Huddled against a block wall
a ragged man waits for warmth
seeking sunshine strength—
not even a shopping cart
for protection.

No hint of yesterday's gloom, when
everything was shades of gray
so damp you felt it on your face—
tree tips dripped onto wet earth,
houses, bushes, barns, appeared
mysteriously out of the mist
as we crept slowly down the road
seeking familiar landmarks . . .
sudden surprise of oncoming vehicle
quickened pulse and grip on wheel,
longing to be home and safe.

CHAD SOKOLOVSKY

Chad Sokolovsky's poetry has appeared in *Penumbra, Stanislaus Connections, Song of the San Joaquin, Quercus Review,* and *Naked Knuckle* to name a few. He is also a competing slam poet and a founding member of the slam poetry duo "Comma Sutra." He was nominated for a Pushcart Prize in 2010 and currently resides in Modesto.

"I was born in San Francisco and lived in the Bay Area until I moved to Modesto at the age of 18. The physical landscape of the orchards, vast sky, and near by foothills of the Valley have always held something special for me. There's a connection to the landscape that both keeps people who pay attention to it grounded, and fosters an environment of community and creativity that I never experienced living in the city."

STANISLAUS COUNTY

I used to be addicted
to the crossword
and syrupy coffee,
the avalanche
of raw sugar boulders
tumbling into a mug
and watching old Jim
dump salt like hail
on poached eggs.

Someone started planting
tract homes over almond tree
roots, while the dust
of old farm stories
still settled into the grease-
grimed tables.
I used to pray back then
before I migrated
to a shoebox in Berkeley,

where no one
does the crossword
and coffee only comes
in a scalding paper cup,
where I can't forget
the 110 degree summers
building tomato pallets
in Ceres and struggling
to sleep where the sidewalks
still blister at midnight.

GREEN THUMB

This afternoon is oozing
through the faded plank decking
of the Queen Bean cafe,
and I should be home
pulling weeds from the backyard.
The ones that have taken off their shoes
and made themselves quite comfortable
on the moist mattress of my garden bed.

Wind-blown seeds we can't even see
burrow into our skin and sprout
relatives and acquaintances
we didn't ask for. I only remember
planting lavender, pink camellias,
and azaleas, but spend more time
trying to extract the impacted roots
of random people that have nestled
into my head like wisdom teeth.

Like the woman who's wheezing
from an asthma attack
as she rifles through her tired canvas purse
for a Virginia Slim and an absent match.
Her white knuckles clutching
between aching breasts, she grips her chest
as if it was going to dart in front of a bus
and asks Ed for a light.

I don't understand her orange crocs
or the pink and white plaid capris
that have seen better days,
or why I even notice her
and the other nomads
that frequent this place.

If only they knew
how much I tend to them,
how familiar the prickly veins
of their rough, jagged leaves
are to my fingers, or
how carefully I release
their dandelion limbs
into the wind.

WHY I WRITE AT COFFEE SHOPS

Because I get nowhere
writing in my living room.
Like trying to run in dreams,
my rubbery insect legs sludging
through dripping tree sap.
It's the possibility of seeing something
that wasn't meant to be poetic:
a lit cigarette flicked
across the sidewalk sparking
off a navy blue fender,
shadows evolving across a white wall,
or the city exhaling through a man-hole
cover on J Street. As if I'm
waiting to see the one perfect image
that will lead me towards the last line
of a poem that's just out of reach:
like a child jumping in slow motion
to catch a yellow balloon
rising in the September wind.

SILENT KILLER

I held mom's hand until I was eight
because the man with a peppered mustache
and a dented Ford station wagon
was swiping boys from the sidewalks
of Concord. Back then the Zodiac Killer
was still stalking in the gardenias
of Golden Gate Park. Death lurked
on milk cartons, orphaned fliers

stapled to telephone poles, Ouija boards,
chef's knives and unmarked white plastic
bottles breathing beneath the sink.
I would lie beneath Star Wars sheets
afraid that I swallowed a Lego.
But somehow Death's crooked
finger never quite reached the backseat
the way mom's backhand or dad's

frustration could. Never as close
to home as a leather belt
coiled in the dresser's top drawer
or a wooden spoon crouched
at the bottom of a purse.
None as lethal as the suffocating
silence between fathers and sons
that I swallowed like cyanide.

I NEVER LIKED BOLOGNA

or the London Broil mom scorched
in the electric oven with a broken thermostat.
I hated the clockwork regularity
of Friday night tacos,
shredded cheddar in dull Tupperware
bowls, or corn tortillas
saturated in Mazola. I don't remember
much from Concord, or the apartment
in San Francisco across from the bakery.
But I liked it when she cut my hair
over the kitchen's criss-cross linoleum,
avocado bath towel draping my shoulders
while Neil Diamond serenaded us Holly Holy
from the living room.

I turned 36 this year,
scarred two tattoos into my back
and argued with my daughter
about the length of bangs
swooping across her glasses.
It's not that I want to be 13 again,
pimples cratering my forehead
or the complicated geography of braces.
I just miss the wonder sometimes-

> the milky mystery of my first orgasm,
> the dry crackle and pale blue smoke
> of that first cigarette behind the garage,
> imagining the complicated mechanics
> of braziers or if the moon's full face
> ever noticed us praying.

I was 18 the last time mom cut my hair,
her arthritis claiming a knick of hair
behind my ear. I miss the closeness

of her fingers soft as ripe pear flesh
against my scalp and the textured
orange floor of that old kitchen.
It was the only time I ever talked
to her about girls and she just listened.
Maybe it was the sharp slice of crisp
scissors trimming dirty blonde follicles
or that I never looked her in the eye
when I finally understood she wasn't
going to get better or that we would
never be as close as those afternoons
when I confessed I didn't believe in God
and she pretended not to hear me.

ELIZABETH SOUSA

Elizabeth Sousa is a survivor, a mother, and a child of several movements, therefore a poet. She is a regular at Modesto's monthly poetry slam, Slam on Rye (where she has managed to win once or twice), and has been published in *Collected Whispers*.

"The Central Valley is my new playground after a lifetime of romping about the East Bay, although twenty-seven years is hardly a lifetime. I would've never predicted that my daughter and I would settle in the Modesto area among its sneeze-inducing agriculture. It was just as unexpected to find that it would be here that my love for the arts would be nurtured. A year ago I stumbled upon what I thought was some sort of underground culture, my first poetry slam. Before Slam on Rye, writing had just been a means to interpret and endure life. I was ignorant to the existence of a poetry scene, let alone how vast it was and how powerful it could be. The native poets I have had the honor of observing have been incredible influences, mentors even, and have encouraged my passion to read, write,

grow, and better my community. For me, there is much yet to learn from Modesto, but so far I am thankful for the surprising inspiration drawn from the calming structure of its budding crops, the bustle of the locals downtown, and all of the rich history that saturates this region."

DIAMONDS

Don't give me diamonds.
Give me the diamonds that wink
on the surface of late-afternoon waves.
I can float with my eyes closed
listening to the sound of them
caressing this rocky shore.
Tuck me under these cotton candy clouds
and kiss me like the sun upon my skin.

Give me your love for today so abundantly
that it may spill over into tomorrow
and we could fill this life so full
with yesterdays.
Slither through the crack
of my doorway unannounced
with your breath on my shoulder.
Command me like an Aztec warrior until I collapse
into the small of my back.

Don't give me complacency.
Give me eyes of passion and make love to me
with your words.
Whisk me into your syllables strung like pearls.
I want to swallow your phrases
and hold you for hours inside my paragraph.

You make me feel as beautiful
as a sunset on the horizon
first thing in the morning
with foggy eyes and full lips telling you
I love you.
And when you weave quilts
with the strands of my hair in your fingertips
and I trace the outline of your jaw with mine,
it makes me feel like failing

just to say that I tried.

So don't give me diamonds.
Give me the smile of waking next to me,
give me those moments mundane,
give me awkwardness, and give me growth.
Give me the comfort in knowing
someone
is holding my hand
on the edge of this cliff.

Justin Souza

Justin Souza received his MFA from Cornell University in 2008. He has made his way in the world the last ten years as a creative writing teacher, wine salesman, photographer, copywriter, web designer and farmer, among other professions. His poetic attempts to explore the edges of the American experience have appeared in *Oak Bend Review, Berkeley Poetry Review* and, of course, in *Quercus Review*, among others.

"I'm a Modesto boy born and bred, though for more than ten years I ran away from the Valley, living in liberal oases around the country, as I remained fearful of the place I was born and raised. I'm residing back here now, with a wife (fellow poet and anthology denizen Dana Koster) and a new baby, and I've realized that there was never anything to run away from but me and that Modesto, for all the fundamentalist bugaboo I armed it with, is just a place where people do the best they can with what they have."

A YEAR OUT OF WORK

1

The first month, it's a novelty. It's easy
to hear vacation when your boss says layoffs.
A bending of the vowels, some phonetic massage.
The hard "a" hints at stretching
in bed in the early afternoon, at sunshine,
flowers, waterfalls, birds tuning into pop anthems.
By the second syllable you're already gone.

Halfway through the first week, you laugh it off
when a friend asks leaning in *how are you doing?*
her emphasis clinging like a drowning cat to the last word
you have savings, you have options, you have time
what seems like golden endless time ahead of you
waiting to be filled with everything
you've wanted and never gotten to.
You'll be fine. This is a good thing. Really.
And if you start to worry   why would you?
but if you do, you know you can just pick up a job
somewhere

you've been here before, you say,
there are always jobs

2

By the second month, the time you wanted starts
to overwhelm you. You take up a hobby
pottery, woodworking,
something that occupies your hands
keeps you moving, off the couch
something completely unlike your career

go into it like a bull breaking through a fence
stay up late every night reading up, studying

you'll master in a month what has taken centuries to develop
you'll rewrite history

you spend your days making
amateurish mistakes you don't understand
a tableful of rough pots, a half dozen crooked birdhouses,
specialized equipment standing in the corners of your room

every three or four days, force yourself to look for jobs
at the risk of catching a glimpse
of how far this goes

3
Burn through one ream of paper printing resumes
start in on another. Follow up
on openings for dishwashers, sign wavers,
unskilled labor. Statistically, twenty percent
of the people you know should be out of work.
In reality, it's more like half.

4
You used to pay rent without thinking
now it takes a week's accumulated fortitude
just to sign the check

savings it took you years to build dwindle every day
when did everything get so expensive? how
is it possible you've never noticed?

you spend half your time cutting corners
canceling magazines, cable, hours on hold with the bank
waiting out the credit card companies,
the government help line

halfway through the month, you decide
name brand mayonnaise doesn't taste two dollars better
you're not too proud to wear a coat indoors

you don't love this apartment as much as you thought

5
you move back in with your parents

7
you become the stone in the water
moon and sun streak the sky, a fragile spasm of light
unspooling like ribbon from the horizon
storm clouds form and fade, rain begins to fall
you hardly sleep

you turn pages
to look at every word of a novel without reading one
you cannot think of anyone else to call
and it is five in the morning already
though you have not yet realized night has fallen

how long eight hours seemed once,
now you hardly seem to move at all before it is gone
how much giving up you thought there was in working
how much giving in there is in stillness

10
you write endless lists
post-its bristle like quills on your computer monitor
form a pastel beard on your double in the bathroom mirror

bills that must be paid. bills that can wait another month.
what can be sold. what you need to survive.
what to say when people ask.

unemployment sans depression is a masquerade
hopefulness is all body language, cadence; deflection
is mostly fudged statistics, leading questions;
complete success is invisibility
always staying out of sight.

12
You can see from here the edges
of the agreement that makes us men.
You feel yourself move toward the moment
when you decide again who you are.

You think another year of this
and you'll know finally what it means.
Another year of this you will be ready
to give in.

realize
every minute of unemployment since the first
you've been trying
to determine what's worse
pushing on with no hope
or quitting for good.

FALLUJAH STATION

I
The city floats like an island
of garbage in the heat.
The sliver moon skittish
as a bomber shivers
up from the skyline, dust
pools against the horizon.
You will not believe
this is the end of days, you vow
you see something past it.

II
Through the acetylene haze you count
the lost, bend their names
through your mouth: Juan,
whose grandmother told the papers
he was a good boy and did not say
his temper after kept her always in fear.
Andres who broke apart under it
and shot two men and himself
on the street in Ceres.
Daniel who went missing
and didn't turn up for a year,
dead in a mass grave
on the edge of the desert.

III
Newscasters stop
to tell me I've got it all wrong.
Reports just released from our affiliates
indicate there is no war, dead
people you thought you knew
live across town in rained out
bungalows, there is no world
beyond our borders, there is no pain

but God's. We will give you new realities.
Give me disregard.

IV
The sun droops like a starving dog
on the horizon. Men clot
at the ridgetops, pray. In the glare
the weapons in their hands look
for a moment like boughs
drooping with blossoms

V
Recruiters muscle through the phone lines
to all the high school kids
who have nothing planned, Do
You Know Where You're Going
With Your Life? Have You Ever
Thought About A Career As A Hero?
All over the country men are rising
to do their duty. Old glory
is buying new blood from the street.
I can tell you everything there is to know
about destruction.

Let me tell you about America.

VI
This is the world
ending. Not in darkness or sound
but in static. Death tolls
meaningless as lottery jackpots
between reality shows, ads
for used cars, fast food
wan blue light edging
every window in every town.

Tiny flares of grief slipping
unnoticed into the stars.

VII
Somewhere else from everywhere
kids you never thought to know
trying as hard as they can to prove something
anything, dying alone.

GARY THOMAS

Gary Thomas taught language arts for thirty-plus years at Turlock Junior High and English for seven years as an adjunct instructor at Modesto Junior College; at both venues, he introduced, read, memorized, shared, and taught poetry every day. He is lucky enough to be a charter member of the Central Valley writing group known as Licensed Fools. He has been published in such journals as *Penumbra, California English, CLiPs, ZamBomba!, TalkArts, In the Grove, hardpan,* and *Snail Mail Review.*

"I grew up on a peach farm just outside Empire, CA, and attended Empire Union School, Downey High, MJC, and Stanislaus State College. In what I write, I still *live* on that farm, in Modesto suburbs of my imagining, and now in Turlock and some sort of exosphere. As an elementary school student, I wrote poetry secretively (boys weren't supposed to write poetry.) In high school, I wrote bad love poems and anguished folk-music broadsides against the Military Industrial Complex. At MJC, I had the great good fortune and blessing to have Lee Nicholson as my creative writing

teacher, and later, as my ongoing poetry inspiration. The Modesto Arch continues to be my poetic focal point because of Lee Nicholson; every time I pass through it, I am grateful for Lee and all other clear-eyed/voiced local poets."

THE SAME

We kid ourselves: this is the same
porch, familiar white rail,

view of constant clouds, wind
brushing cedar boughs, eggs

breaking into red scrambling bowl
in the too-small kitchen.

The news, the news, the news
still tells us all is

war, craters, broken levees.
In the unabridged dictionary in the den,

misery still has the same letters, and
our dentist sends us happy yellow reminders

of our next hygiene appointment. Traffic
lights on our street are synchronized.

But the crow sits on a different branch
this morning, complaining

or bragging in a different timbre. The lawn
has a new fairy ring. Someone is singing

nearby; the old tune catches us by surprise.

FERN LOVE

They mate like ghosts, underneath
what the overworld witnesses and ignores,
reaching for each other sporadically
as their common breezes tell them
It is time now.
They are not delicate.
Otherwise,
what astute botanical voyeur would have
named one of their kinship *Leather Leaf,*
and another *Sword?*
It is true
they welcome their sister, *Rosy Maidenhair,*
but only because she would blush deeper
if they did not, and she knows
all their stories, all their unchaste secrets.
So long as clear water stays
long enough inside dark loam,
no act, no position is unnatural,
each midsummer evening is eternally
a dance of will and wisp,
stem begets frond,
life unfurls above
from what gropes beneath,
and there is always time for that.

SONNET CATCH XXII FROM THE PAPUESE

—after J. Heller and E. B. Browning

When our two spirits drift at last between
the grin of moon, chagrin of spring's full sun,
winking, shimmering, mousy hair undone,
our sainted Margaret Mead, free love's queen,
shall break into fire, bid us be obscene
but not heard in the flames we will have spun.
If angels' only ecstasy is one
doxology after another, lean
closer, my dark love—let us be well-damned
as we do our earthly joys consummate,
as we don't pretend we are not enjambed
in our contrarious conjoined checkmate,
eager to be islands undiagrammed,
sweating spirits gods dare not isolate.

Bryce Thornburg

Bryce Thornburg's work has appeared in *Quercus Review* and *CLAM*. He is a winner of the *Poetry for the Mind's Joy* contest, a national initiative by former Poet Laureate Kay Ryan to promote poetry on community college campuses. He is currently pursuing degrees in English and linguistics at University of California, Berkeley.

"The truth is I don't really know Modesto that well. I've never actually *lived* here. I was born here, sure, but most of my childhood was spent bouncing between my divorced parents' homes in Ceres and Manteca. It wasn't until I was a student at Modesto Junior College that I would spend much time here at all. I began my stint there as a computer science major. It took a while before I would realize that literature was what I was really after, and it wasn't some all-at-once, head-over-heels love affair, but rather something slow growing. But that's the point of the place, I think—or at least a part of it. I may have showed up pretty confused and directionless, but I was surrounded by intelligent and supportive people who allowed me to make my own choices. My relationship with Modesto has largely been one of passing through—from my ricocheting up and down Highway 99 to my education at MJC—and I still think of it that way; everything I have held onto and the ways in which I have changed are just re-enactments of that same returning that I have been doing for years."

I LIKE TO WATCH LATE NIGHT TALK SHOWS

I don't do it for the way the host stands
on the balls of his feet, hands
in pockets jingling invisible keys,
shrugging off joke after joke
after newspaper headline, the
trickles of prompted laughter from
the hidden audience.

I don't do it for the band,
that mass of sunglasses-at-night
men at attention,
wrangling gnarled tubes of brass,
the big grin of the Letterman-toothed
keyboard, the drummer adrift
in a sea of symbols, taut skin,
gleaming metal.

I don't do it for the guest,
elegant, refined, pushing the best book
ever written, the best movie ever
produced, stationed upon
a couch that seems out of place.

I watch these nighttime routines for
the commercials. Well, not the
commercials themselves,
but for that moment when the host
submits to the advertisements,
and the camera pans out, the
roar of the attendees and
groove of the band drowning out
the voices of host and guest.
They lean forward, in a silent huddle,
mouthing to one another
as I strain to hear the host through

the static dust of my television,
wondering what secrets he is telling
when the microphone is cut,
and he is expected, for once, not to be so
damn funny.

PIRATES ARE RHOTIC

Singing to is singing at
But overheard
Songs for anyone nearby

No soap radios full of laughs
You are the butt of
The jokes overhead

And bit by bit
It's a case
Of staircase wit

Outrage like pissing in the
dark
Somewhat difficult
Until it's suggested you sit.

LILLIAN VALLEE

Lillian Vallee teaches English at Modesto Junior College. Her most recently published poems and prose appear in *The Cosmopolitan Review*, *The Invisible Rope*, and *The Devil's Punchbowl*. She writes a monthly column, "Rivers of Birds, Forests of Tule: Central Valley Nature & Culture in Season," for *Stanislaus Connections*.

"I came to Modesto as a free-lance translator and writer, and the first poem I wrote here was "Commuter Daybreak" because that was my life: rising before dawn and seeing other people already hard at work in fields and orchards. Yet even as I was wrenching myself away from my children in the early morning hours, the poignant beauty of the San Joaquin River and the Diablo Range consoled me. The telluric powers of this place are strong and they have insinuated themselves into my imagination. I fell in love with the La Loma neighborhood and have never looked back. Modesto has been my lookout and entry into everything deep: history, time, song. I don't idealize Modesto; the city's problems and tensions are real but not insurmountable. I cannot, however, separate Modesto from the San Joaquin Plain or the Great Central Valley bioregion in which they are located. I was lucky to have had as a mentor Polish poet Czeslaw Milosz who made me understand the hardships of the writing life, its sacrifices and obligations, and to him I am indebted for the tools I use to make sense of the historical moment and the biotic community in which I find myself."

TRANSFUSION

When I was an infant, my mother tells me
My ear became infected, my brain inflamed
And the postwar blood of my Polish parents
Was too weak to repel the assault—
Something wanted me dead
Something small but powerful

They filled my veins with the blood
Of a German soldier whose views on the
Inferiority of the Slavic races remain unknown
Something wanted me alive
Something small but more powerful
Than whatever wanted me dead

UNINVITED

Because it would have been ungrateful
Because it would have been ungracious
I did not ask in the ornate ballroom
On whose backs was it built
I did not ask but everyone knew
Whose backs, whose backs were lashed
Before they were fed at the cattle troughs
Whose backs, sturdy though they might have been
For a dollar a day, a guzzle on Saturday
They whizzed from the basket into the air
Before they plugged in the dynamite
Shattering the sacred mountain
Shattering the golden mountain
Sierra Nevada in its cape of dawn

Whose backs, I should have shouted, whose guns
Into the drizzle of speeches
About life on the edge
Shots ring out, pronghorn scatter
Tule bull is brought to his knees
A grizzly rises for one last look
"Almost nothing is not yet nothing,"
Utters the sage
Let's give ourselves a hand
While pelicans circle over cotton
Looking, looking for Tulare Lake

Whose backs in the doorway are watching
So no one will nab the art work
Of Dutch Masters, Medieval altars
Piano music, piano
Whose backs, oh really woman
Piano, the wine's not bad
Whose backs in the chain gangs—hush
Whose children in the vineyards—hush

Whose guns from on horseback—hush
Hush
Hush

I CANNOT ESCAPE YOU

You are like the air
in this aquarium of earth
Like the sun on these darkening days
Like the first notes
Of a song I cannot remember
Like a cairn on a mountain trail
 a bear box keeping the food safe
 a nesting box nailed not too high up
 so the nestlings don't have too far to fall
You are everywhere now
in every leaf and needle
in every dank decaying thing
in all my helplessness, stupidity,
dullness, intensity
some soft small light shines

HYMN

After the highest point, the dip, curve to the south
And I am all yours, Mother. The moon lays
Her infant light into this cradle, then scatters
A handful of coins into the San Joaquin
Slumbering grasses nuzzle the loam
While cottonwood and oak, elderberry and willow
Toss their manes in their sleep
Like wild horses pawing the channel
I would have thought my heart too small
To contain the unbridled banks of the river
I would have thought the world too bereft
Of tenderness, to fill this trough so full

HEAT, OR SMALL BOMB OF REVELATION
A POEM IN THIRTEEN TORRENTS: SECOND TORRENT

"Learn to wear exotic masks—but not to hide anything." —Thomas E. Mails

1.
You learn that the number eight—
Your number in the Zodiac, Scorpio—
Is the one you had mistaken for bad luck.
This time its two bellies, like a snowman's,
Bring you a searing, coal-eyed joy

I wish I could separate him
From the smell of sweet grass
Or the South Dakota sage
He gathered along the banks
Of the Cheyenne River before
They cut his body, before
He bundled the stalks, tied them
With a red strip to his ankle.
This he brought to me
And it felt like my body
Was being pierced and I
Was being tethered to some
Arching tree, struggling to
Get loose before the flesh tore.

I crawl into his bed
To smell his sweat
Because his absence is sweeter
More manageable than
His mocking eyes. I
Cannot say he is delicate.
He has slept too much
With the wind for that.

His hands are rough, his
Movements direct, he
Has not learned from
The birds. He accepts
Without thanks or guilt
Or obligation and gives
In the same way, without
Expectation. He is patient
With his appetites. He talks
And mimics and clowns
To cover his tracks.

Is it my own detachment
I see in him? A mirror image
So disarming and exact in
Two seconds I am at the core
Of the earth, red hot magma.

The fire, the fire, the fire.
The fear, the fear, the fear.

"I'll make you work to know me,"
He says, and I don't know what
To make of this, what to watch
For. "You don't have to be the
Rock of Gibraltar, you know," and
My mind races, Rock of Gibraltar?
A colony, a fortress on a narrow
Promontory, a person with strength
And endurance, someone who can be
Relied on to block the entrance
To a coveted sea, but I was thinking
Scylla and Charybdis, a cliff and a
Maelstrom, a lovesick girl
Dragged through the water by her feet,

Odysseus tied "hard in hurtful bonds"
To the mast, and the honey sweet
Voices that draw every reckless ship
To the rocks.

2.
I can't get anything done
Done: what is this *done*?
I saw a jay this morning
Peck at a branch until it
Fell away and now he could
Get the acorn, even though
It was still green.
When the sun strikes
The pool, the purple ball,
The white sage, even the
Green plastic turtle sandbox,
I know I must break with
The old life. You dream
Of a silver fish with
One black eye staring into
infinity—death, my mother
Would say, but what is dying,
Mother? What is dying?
The season? The body?
This mind? Is the old love
decaying with the rotting leaves?
There is so much to do
And I can get nothing done.
I can hardly move my
Feet to imitate walking.
I feed people
I let them sleep in my house
I make them soothing teas
I let them sleep with me
Well, just one to be exact.
And then the overwhelming

Grief. Drink to its dregs
This mortal chalice, this
Heady drug, this blood of
Another heart, pulsing,
Undemanding, waiting
For a sign. This gift,
This sunlit, swaying gift.

3.
When the garden lights up in the morning
And there are melons and chocolate
Left from the night before, and
The smell of coffee and bacon from
The rising before dawn, and almonds
Are laid on a tarp to dry, I
Search and search for words to
Express this whirling, purple ball
Of happiness. We don't need to
Talk. We don't need to see or
Smell the other. The floor creaks,
The door pops ajar, and in
Comes the hurricane. Red ribbons
Adorn the oak. He has the face
Of a grandfather. Below are
Butts crushed by feet nervous
With late night conversations.
Your breast is split open like
That feral chicken's the hawk
Or raccoon took one morning
And you see them still, the magpies,
The messengers pecking with relish
At the exposed heart: ah, there it is:
Your nightmare, your chasm, your abyss.

4.
I couldn't start before
And now I can't stop

If there were just one poem
I would call it "September Rise"
Because snow is still melting
In the mountains
Because snow is still watering
The dessicated plain
I call out for something
I cannot name
Two hollows at the thigh bones
Something arching and crossing
In a vault
I could blame it
On the imagination
If my body
Were not complicit
If it were not smoking
Like some smoldering herb
Red embered when you blow on it
Why is this given?
Why do I ask so
Many questions?
Why can't I just lean
Into the current?
Because I have been wracked
On broken rocks in the river
Because I have lost
Shoes and hats
And almost a child once
I have walked
For miles in the heat
And been ferried across
By drunken revelers
I step carefully
Into every water body
Believing it will buoy
Me up but worried
Nonetheless about the
Long sinewy grasses

In the lakes and the
Barbed wire of fish traps.

5.
This voice is unfamiliar to me
Its raspiness, its deep tickle and quiver
I eat bacon and sausage for breakfast
Scorn the quinoa for now. The purple ball
glides around the edge of the round pool
keeping time, spinning like the earth
if it were not for its bar code to
remind me of the price, the price.
Your bed is too big for one person
Your poetry is too safe for two.
I am in a wreck every morning
And drag myself out of a burning cage.

I would thank Sweet Jesus if
I thought he had anything to do with it
But it is really Mary who kept
The secret of how sweetly Jesus was made
Even God has his weaknesses
As long as there is one hummingbird
Stirring the lavender fronds
As long as there is one obnoxious jay
Pecking open walnuts at four a.m.
I will love you
The continent of you
The history of you
The backbreak of you
The unknit wound of you
The hustling mouth
The smoky prayer
The unremovable tattoo of you

6.
Is this an illness?
Or is this what has been missing?

What all great art reaches for?
A doorway out of confusion

If not for the hummingbird
At the throat of so many fuchsia flowers
I would be struck dumb by my own disarray
It searches every bloom for what it needs
And then rests on a branch awhile
Thankful, I think, for
The fuchsia going to seed
For its long, red throat,
Its filaments
The profusion of cavities
On just one stem

7.
On what is love *built*?
Is it *built* at all?
What is strange, remote
Suddenly has you
In its rousing embrace
How does love *work*?
Does it *work* at all?
Or does it run its hands
Along your see-through blouse
Finding your lines?
Why does love matter?
Why not just pleasure?
And pleasure giving?
Why must the anchor be set
In a dark place inhabited
By things that don't have eyes?
Why does he look so different in a cap?
The head bare is large, stark
Like a temple carving
From a time when hearts
Were cut away
With obsidian knives

And placed
Still warm and beating
On the altar.

GILLIAN WEGENER

Gillian Wegener is the author of *Lifting One Foot, Lifting the Other* (In the Grove Press, 2001) and *The Opposite of Clairvoyance* (Sixteen Rivers Press, 2008). Widely published, she was awarded top honors in the 2006 and 2007 Rosenberg Poetry Prize. Originally from Queens, NY, she teaches junior high English in Oakdale and lives in Modesto where she hosts the monthly 2nd Tuesday Reading Series at the Barkin' Dog.

"When I first moved here from Humboldt County, I couldn't breathe in the heat. I was mind-numbingly lonely. So, I turned to poetry. I'd written on and off since I was a teenager, but suddenly poetry became essential. The Valley was not beautiful to me then. It was brown and heat-stunned, and I learned quickly that if I was going to find any beauty, I would have to focus on the details. Here was a small brown bird chasing a hawk. Here was the perspective of telephone lines disappearing down a rural road and a rancher's weathered face reflected in his side-view mirror. Here was the crush of full canals and the dust on the windows of the abandoned Woolworth's on 10th Street. Eventually, I did find my footing, did learn to breathe, and did find people, generous and kind people, who saw this place as beautiful in ways I didn't and who could and did open up those vistas to me with their friendship and their poetry. In spite of myself, this place became home."

STORM WARNING

Our bodies are inadequate shelters, lean-tos in typhoons.
Our hearts need so much more than this scant housing,
the cage of porous bone, the thin blanket of skin.
       Every single storm
rocks the heart as if it has been left exposed to the elements:
struck by lightning, battered by wind, drowning
again and again in whatever sediment rushes past,
the familiar surge of water closing in, the sinking down.
Some days there is no storm, but there is still no safety, no shelter
from the sun. It shines, warm and warm, and without warning
the burn sets in, sneaks in and blisters us before we realize it.
The heart knows no safe place for rest, trapped as it is in a body
it is not always pleased to call home. But what to do?
Arthur cloaked his knights in armor and still they carried
their wounded, mortal hearts within themselves, days passing
heavily in downpourings of rain and thunder. Each moment
for us threatens another squall. Or the promise of sunlight.
       The weather
is unpredictable, but the heart has never learned this.
       What the heart has learned
is that sometimes in the darkness, in the warmth between storms,
the stars come out and, for a moment, everything is perfect.

ANOTHER APOCALYPTIC SIGN

The sign reads *Jesus Is Coming Quickly*
and I imagine Jesus coming on the run
down the main street at rush hour.
He's never learned to drive, so there he is
with his robes flapping behind him, his feet
beating the hot pavement, unsandaled and wounded.
He wears no watch, but he has somewhere
to be and he is already later than he'd like.
See that little furrow of worry between his eyes?
Drivers don't know what to make of him.
He doesn't bother with sidewalks or bike paths,
so there is some swerving in and out of traffic.
Brake lights slam and flash. Someone honks.
Most folks think he's just another crazy, but
they'll realize their mistake soon enough.
After all, there must be a reason Jesus is coming
quickly, to this town, at this moment, charging
across the intersection even before the light turns green.

EGGSHELLS

At first we just find a few eggshells in the corners.
We are careful not to step on them. We pick them up,
sweep them up. We take them out with the trash,
but soon they are everywhere. The rug is covered with them.
The seats of chairs, even the window sills shimmer all curve
and fragility. Oh be careful, be careful. A misstep will fracture,
will crush. Look how delicate. We admire their mystery,
but there is no place to stand and no place to sit, and when
we walk, no matter how careful we are, eggshells are smashed and
drive their fine daggers into the soles of our feet in this house
where the broom to sweep up the ruined shells
is soon worn to nothing.

OWL SIGHTING

Each morning we'd search
for the small pellets of bone and fur and tail
in the scruffy grass under that palm, unfortunate
mice who'd become her solitary meal.
And we'd find them…

bone turned almost the color
of the late summer grass, fur scraps the color
of the neglected dirt. Odd treasures, but proof
our ghost was up there, in her palm palace, proof that
she'd come home again.

And that was what we wanted.
Hungry from all the nights we could hear her call,
the long, whoo-whoo bouncing off stucco and asphalt
and down to us who'd point and wonder
if she were here or in that tree there,
until finally,

we'd make ourselves still under a sky gone
so deeply blue, you could taste it on your lips, and
we'd wait, the grass crunching under our shoulders, and
wait, the moon rising from behind the mountain, and wait,
knowing we'd be called in soon, and wait, holding our
breaths and then

she'd launch from her nest all at once. No rustling
to alert us, not ever the shiver of moonlit fronds. And
for a split-second
she'd be closer than any of us would have liked. What if we
stood up and reached? But there was never time to try. She'd
launch herself out to the west and away and away,
this massive winged shadow,

and if one of us blinked,
she'd be gone, and we'd only know by the sharp
intakes of breath around us, but if we saw her go,

even then we'd wonder if we'd dreamed it
maybe; we'd doubt what we'd seen

                              because
it really seemed impossible, this kind of beauty,
living here in our own tree, in our own yard,
so lovely in the sudden moment of its departure, this
shadow bird, this twilight ghost, this remedy
against another cloistered suburban night.

THIS SWEET HAPHAZARD

No one calls this town pretty.
Not with the dusty oleanders off the freeway
and the ragged fenceboards of backyards
propped up with two-by-fours, and
the canals with their twin lies of slow and safe,
and the ash trees, dead branches dangling, and
the large pale no-one's-home houses and
the foreclosed houses and the small houses
with their carefully tended geranium borders,
with the plum trees gone overripe and sticky.
No one calls this town pretty with the heat
rippling off the parking lots and the sighs
of aunts and uncles sitting in the shade of garages
filled with cars that were once meant to go places,
and the church marquee scolding that
Jesus Did Not Read Porn, and the swarms
of mosquitoes buzzing the standing water
from the leaking sprinkler heads in the park.
And yea, no one calls this town pretty
as the creek laps at its share of shopping carts,
and the untended grasses bleach dry by April,
and the public pools are mostly closed,
but the sky here turns indigo on summer nights,
and the hummingbird chases the sparrow
from the feeder, and the kids on the soccer field
run as fast as kids anywhere, oblivious
to the town around them, because after all,
it isn't so bad. It's an okay town.
We know where all the roads go,
and we know where to get good coffee,
and we know what time the train pulls through.
We know too we're more than soil, more than sky,
more than what you've read in the news,
and no, it isn't pretty, but we still live here and
tonight the moon will rise, almost full,
over this sweet haphazard of home.

Kathleen West

Kathleen West wrote poetry as a kid, but stopped at about age 18 and did not start again until she was over 30. Through taking poetry-writing classes with Patrice Vecchione, she started again and has a small collection of poems from the last 25 years.

"I am an Episcopal priest. My husband and I moved to Modesto in August of 2009 so that I could be an assistant priest at St. Paul's Episcopal Church. From Advent (December) 2009 through Pentecost (June) 2010, I led a class at church called 'Poetry Through the Church Year.' We published poems written in those classes in our church newsletter. Then Modesto poets Ed and Roberta Bearden came to church one Sunday in the fall of 2010, and I ended up connecting with them and their poetry-writing group. So Modesto has been an inspiration to me to write poetry because of the people I have met here. They are open and creative and reflective. I have lived the greater portion of my life in Glendale, a Los Angeles suburb. I also spent nine years in Salinas (where I met Patrice). My husband and I spent three years, 2006-09, in Provo, UT. But it is Modesto that has been the most poetry-oriented place. I am constantly being asked now to attend a writing group, write a poem for the next meeting, and submit poems for anthologies. How wonderful this is, and unexpected."

HUMBLE MIRACLES

Early, early these many mornings
the weight of the world on our backs
we have staggered up the stairs
to face those cold pronouns
soberly; fatalistic

like monks pacing a labyrinth
you have traced
meticulous formulas,
mastered esoteric discrepancies.

What is to be the reward
for such perseverance?
Could I ever convince you
of any intrinsic value
in participles—I am afraid
it would be useless to try.

In the wash of weeks,
the flurry of seasons
we plodded together
with lowered eyes

vaguely aware
of the humble miracles
we stepped over delicately
like clusters of mushrooms
half-hidden in dead leaves.

TWILIGHT PUDDLE

Staring into a mud hole
I felt OK, at home,
Part pilgrim
Thinking of that
Warm, glad-faced baby
Who toddles around this yard
In awe of the colors, the space

The breeze was cool and sweet
The ache in my belly calmed

The mud hole becomes a crystal ball
Revealing, sorting, prisming

I saw a tiny burbling in the
Stillness of the
Twilight puddle:
Embryos of poems
Scratch and churn in the darkness.

BRIAN WRIGHT

Brian Wright has been a high school English teacher for thirty-one years. He earned a BA in English from California State University Stanislaus and an MA in English and Creative Writing from San Francisco State University. His interest in poetry caught momentum while serving in the U.S. Navy, flourished in college, and found encouragement from family, friends, teachers and students along the way.

"When thinking about the Modesto area and its influence on my writing life, people mostly come to mind, groups of people and individuals who have influenced or inspired me. Years ago it was a group of poets at Stanislaus State. It was *Big Moon*, and later the poets who gravitated to California Poets in the Schools. It continues to be students, teachers, professors, poets, friends and family. It comes from a sense of competition, collaboration, and dedication to art that exists wherever creative spirits gather."

I SAW HER ALMOST

Driving north in December
after a light rain and overcast
the pavement wet and shining
I saw things along the highway—

first a shoe and then another shoe
then a blue plaid flannel bathrobe
one work glove, a Lakers jersey
number 24 and three white socks.

Then by chance I saw her almost
invisible motionless by the roadside
wearing a red dirty nylon jacket, blue jeans
and at her feet a big plastic bag overflowing.

CULL CANYON

The hills
outside my hometown
were a playground,
the neighborhood kids
sliding down grassy slopes
on cardboard
or collecting pollywogs
from the creek.
We dug forts
on the hillside
and came home
with poison oak.
I remember
Wolverton's farm
and getting permission
to hunt lizards
in the Eucalyptus grove
above their home.
How a skink
could scurry into the bushes,
not as easy to catch
as a blue belly
or as scary
as an Alligator lizard,
leaving its tail with us.
King snakes, Gopher snakes,
squirrels, sparrows,
Redwing Blackbirds and
Bluegills in the lake,
A childhood list
of adventures
within walking distance
of our block.
The last time
I was there,
the canyon
stood shadowed

in memories—
so many streets
and houses
surround it.

Kathleen Wright

Kathleen Wright holds an AA in English studies. She is a mother of three grown children and a grandmother of two amazing grandsons. Her written works have appeared in *MeterMaid Anthology* 2009 and in *Serendipity Poets of Cheyenne's Journal* 2010. She currently is working on her first self-published book of poetry, "Of Sand and Paper," available winter 2011.

"I am resilient and passionate about not allowing life's circumstances to define who I am. I moved to Modesto in 2005, and in 2007, I began my quest at the age of forty-five to complete my education. It was during this time at MJC, when a renewed energy and vigor revealed my innate desire to express life's sensory impressions in poetic form. I enjoy readings at the Second Tuesday Poetry events at the Barkin' Dog and look forward to being a future part of Modesto's artistic community."

THE SEED INSIDE

The ruby fingerlings of tender petals,
reach for the oozed blackness
    of a still night.
The last rays of light tickle the
inner sanctuary of an ever-closing prism.
Dew stems thread off the
persimmon colored moon,
casting images of transparent veins,
    upon your smile.
Stilled by a hushed, whisper
of frozen breath.

DOUG HOLCOMB_____ photographer

Doug Holcomb grew up and still resides in Ceres, California, an agricultural community located in the heart of the Great Central Valley. At age five, Doug bought his first camera for a nickel at an antique auction, but it would take 30 years before he applied himself seriously to the art of photography. Doug's work has been featured in several one-man shows in both Arizona and California, and his work is often found hanging in City Art Gallery in San Francisco. He is the owner of Nine by 9 photography and much of his portrait work can be seen at www.nineby9.com.

"My images are born in the moment. I arrive at my destination and leave with shots I never saw coming. What I end up with is sublimely more important than what I intended. I adapt quickly. A day at the cemetery shooting sullen statues may quickly become a day of sunsets and flora. I follow the images. I don't create them. I find a story in many of my shots, or the stories, I should say, write themselves as I begin to process the photographs. I aim to create strong emotions, wistfulness or vibrancy, sadness or elation, but ultimately it is up to the audience to determine what story each image is meant to tell. For me, that is the best part of art—the connection that is made between the artist and the audience—because their interpretation is as valid as my own. In essence, my intent is not to tell a story, but to inspire one."

acknowledgments

POEMS

Grateful acknowledgment is made to the following publications in which these poems originally appeared. All poems reprinted with permission from their authors.

Karen Hansis Baker: "Pearled Soul" was previously published in *A Common Book of Fools* and the chapbook *Vocal Exercises in Stone* (Rattlesnake Press, 2005).

Sean Barnett: "A Soldier's Thoughts: Before Breakfast" was previously published on Dec. 13, 2010 at blackcatpoems.com.

Ed Bearden: "Relationships" was previously published in *Song of the San Joaquin* Vol. 7, No. 1, Winter 2011. "The Psychotherapist" was previously published in *hardpan*, Vol. 2, No. 1, March 2007.

Roberta Bearden: "A Thousand Miles Away" was previously published in the *California Federation of Chaparral Poets, Inc. Prize Winning Poems, 2006*. "Fog" was previously published in *Song of the San Joaquin*, Vol. 4, No. 1, Winter 2007, and *California Federation of Chaparral Poets, Inc. Prize Winning Poems, 2009*.

Stella Beratlis: "Crop Rows in Autumn" and "Donut Shop at the End of the World" both appeared in *Collision II*.

Elizabeth Coard: "A Small Pink & White Sock" was a contest-winning poem in the Modesto Poets' Corner, 2011. An earlier version of "Roadkill" was previously published in *Penumbra*, Vol. 21.

Tina Arnapole Driskill: An earlier version of "Home Waters" was previously published in *Song of the San Joaquin* Vol. 1, No. 2. Spring 2004.

Cleo Griffith: "Fortune Cookie" was previously published in *Song of the San Joaquin*, Vol. 2 No. 3, Summer 2005. "In the House Without Walls" was previously published in *Hidden Oak*, Spring/Summer 2008. "The Last Dream" was previously published in *Poetry Depth Quarterly*, Fall 2001. "Passing, Passing, Passing By" was previously published in *Poetry Depth Quarterly*, 2006. "The Book of a Thousand Silences" was previously published in *Tiger's Eye*, Spring 2009.

Lynn M. Hansen: "Two Sisters" was previously published in the S*ong of the San Joaquin*, Vol. 7, No. 2, Spring 2010.

Nancy Haskett: "Roller Skates" was winner in the 2009 Modesto Poet's Corner Contest. "William" was previously published in *Poets of the San Joaquin Anthology 2004* and received second place in the Jeannette Gould Maino Contest in 2004.

Lee Herrick: "Salvation" and "Adoption Music" previously appeared in *This Many Miles from Desire* (WordTech Editions, 2007) and "Gardening Secrets of the Dead" was previously published in *The Packinghouse Review*, Vol. 1, No. 1, 2009.

Linda Johnson: "To Tom and Sarah" was previously published in *Song of the San Joaquin* Vol. 7, No. 4, Fall 2010.

Louise Kantro: "Birds Take to the Sky" and "Eleven Hours in a Tornado on the Way to Reno" were previously published in *Dwellingplaces* (Pudding House, 2010).

Dana Koster: "Kablooey" was previously published in *The Cincinnati Review*, Vol. 7, No. 1, Summer 2010.

Debee Loyd: "Juniper Fields" received Honorable Mention at the Berkeley Poets Dinner, 2011.

Arlene Silva Mattos: "Indiscretion" was previously published in the *Honolulu Star-Advertiser*, Dec. 23, 1994.

Paul Neumann: "Aging" was previously published as "Yellow Diamond" in *Forms of Light* (Quercus Review Press, 2003). "San Felipe" was previously published in *Forms of Light*.

Mark Nicoll-Johnson: "Spring Swell" was previously published in *hardpan* Vol. 2, No. 1, March 2007.

Sam Pierstorff: "I Didn't Know They Sold That at the Farmers' Market" was previously published on *Modbee.com,* in *Collision II,* and in *Song of the San Joaquin,* Vol. 5, No. 3, Summer 2008. "It's Okay to Talk to Strangers" is from *Growing Up in Someone Else's Shoes* (World Parade Books, 2010) and premiered as a video poem at the Ill List Poetry Slam Invitational (RyClaps Productions, 2010).

Gordon Preston: "Moonlight" was previously published in *Violins* (Finishing Line Press, 2004)

Linda Gordon Sawyer: "Rules of the Game" won 1st place at the 84th Annual Poet's Dinner 2010 in Oakland.

Chad Sokolovsky: "Stanislaus County" was previously published in *Quercus Review* 2005, *Collision II*, and *Song of the San Joaquin*, Vol. 7, No. 2, Spring 2010. "Why I Write at Coffee Shops" was previously published in *Collision III*. "I Never Liked Bologna" was previously published in *Collision II* and *Quercus Review* 2009. "Silent Killer" was previously published in *Quercus Review* 2010.

Gary Thomas: "The Same" was previously published in *hardpan*, Vol. 1, No. 2, October 2006.

Lillian Vallee: "Transfusion" was previously published in *Periphery,* 8-9 (2002), *The Cosmopolitan Review* and *Collision I*. "Hymn" was previously published in *Stanislaus Connections,* Vol. 2, No. 2, Summer 2010, Nov. 1998.

Gillian Wegener: "Storm Warning" is from her chapbook, *Lifting One Foot, Lifting the Other* (In the Grove Press, 2001). "Another Apocalyptic Sign" is from *The Opposite of Clairvoyance* (Sixteen Rivers Press, 2008). "Owl Sighting" was previously published in *The Packinghouse Review*, Vol. 2, No. 2. "Eggshells" was previously published in *RUNES*, 2006.

PHOTOGRAPHS

Photos of 47 out of 51 poets and all cover images
        by **Doug Holcomb**, *nineby9.com.*

Photo of Kathleen Wright
        by **Robert Eichorst**, *singerstudioandgallery.com.*

Photo of George Rogers
        by **David Rogers** and **Ken White.**

Photo of Lee Nicholson
        courtesy of **Candace Nicholson.**

Photo of Gordon Durham
        courtesy of **James Shuman.**

special thanks

The editors extend a very special thanks to . . .

Claire Zoghb for her amazing cover design skills. **Kimberly Wesson** for assisting Doug Holcomb. **Nancy Haskett** for her prompt and exceptional proofreading skills. **Candace Nicholson** and **Bev Aderholt** for their assistance with photos and poems for Lee Nicholson. **Lynn M. Hansen** for her financial contribution to this anthology on behalf of Lee Nicholson. **Paul Neumann** for his generosity and support. **Tom Myers, Ken White, David Rogers,** and **Gordon Preston** for choosing poems for George Rogers, and **Tom Myers** and **Ken White** for George's biography. **James Shuman** for his help contacting Gordon Durham. **Lillian Vallee** for all her work with the foreword.

The Barkin' Dog Grill, especially Hanibal and Evin Yadegar, for supporting the 2nd Tuesday Poetry Series. **The Prospect Theater**, especially Jack Souza and Kathleen Ennis, for supporting Slam on Rye, Modesto's monthly poetry slam. **The State Theater**, especially Sue Richardson, for supporting the annual Ill List Poetry Slam Invitational. **The Photographers' Gallery**, especially Dave Schroeder and Diane Moody, for supporting "Collision: The Impact of Poetry and Photography."

The English Department at Modesto Junior College, especially Judy Gonzales and Patrick Bettencourt, for supporting Quercus Review Press. **Modesto Junior College, the MJC Foundation, the Chancellor,** and **the YCCD Board of Trustees** for their support of poetry by offering creative writing poetry courses every semester and supporting reading and workshop events with nationally celebrated poets.

The hard-working editors of Modesto's numerous long-running, upstart, and/or recently retired literary magazines where many of these poems previously appeared: *Song of the San Joaquin, Naked Knuckle, Quercus Review, hardpan, Snail Mail Review,* and "A Gathering of Voices" from the monthly publication *Stanislaus Connections.*

The Modesto Bee for its support, publication, and ongoing coverage of poetry in our region. **The City of Modesto** for its support of poetry in the community and the poet laureate program.

Made in the USA
Lexington, KY
22 July 2012